REGIONS OF THE NEW EUROPE

A comparative assessment of key
factors in choosing your location

Third Edition, 1995

**Corporate
Location**

EJ ERNST & YOUNG

CONTENTS

Dedicated to the memory of
Sophie Anne and
Sarah Collette

THE AUTHORS

ERNST & YOUNG

Ernst & Young is a leading international firm of accountants, advisers and consultants with some 66,000 staff in over 125 countries. In Europe it has a network of 320 offices providing a full range of business and financial services. This report has been compiled by Ernst & Young's European Location Advisory Service (ELAS). Through ELAS, Ernst & Young assists clients in selecting locations for regional headquarters, offices, distribution centres, R&D centres and manufacturing plants, by matching their requirements with specific countries, regions and sites. This service covers all the key factors that are relevant when selecting a new location – such as the accessibility of markets and suppliers; the cost and availability of materials; the cost of labour and the skills available; the economic and social infrastructure; logistics; property matters; tax; and government grants. ELAS provides clients with flexible, impartial and comprehensive advice to ensure that location decisions take into account the issues that are important to the client's business and objectives. ELAS also helps to ensure that potentially beneficial options are not overlooked, and that clients' European strategies are successful over the long term.

For further information, contact David Rees, Ernst & Young, Becket House, 1 Lambeth Palace Road, London SE1 7EU, UK, tel +44 171 928 2000, fax +44 171 928 1345, or your local Ernst & Young office.

This book was researched, compiled and written with the aid of Ernst & Young professionals throughout Europe and the United States, especially: Richard Crawford, Mark Hughes, Graham Johnson, Melanie Kill, David Rees, Phil Roberts, Peter Scholes, John Siraut, Derek Smith and Sean Wheeler.

CORPORATE LOCATION

Corporate Location, the bimonthly magazine published by Euromoney Publications PLC, is the core of an organisation which supplies a complete range of services on the specialised topic of inward investment. The magazine provides essential news, views and authoritative analysis on issues of concern for the potential investor, and features in-depth profiles of the major FDI players. It is read by executives in North America, Western Europe and East Asia whose companies may be contemplating an overseas investment. *Corporate Location* also offers information and guidance for development agencies, from marketing personnel training courses to the annual Attracting and Keeping Corporate Investors conference.

For further information, contact Fiona Jebb, editor, Nicholas Duggan, international sales director, or Elizabeth Gaskell, events director, at Nestor House, Playhouse Yard, London EC4V 5EX, UK, tel +44 171 779 8368, fax +44 171 779 8369.

Design: Adam Hay
Editorial Production: Jane Lamacraft
Graphics: Chapman Bounford

CONTACT LIST: ERNST & YOUNG

Austria
Wolfgang Heiling
Ernst & Young
Unternehmensberatung GmbH
Teinfaltstrasse 4
1010 Vienna
tel +43 1 535 4414
fax +43 1 535 4004

Belgium
Jan De Decker
Ernst & Young
Avenue Marcel Thiry 204
B-1200 Brussels
tel +32 2 774 9111
fax +32 2 774 9090

Cyprus
Nikols Lakoufis
Ernst & Young
PO Box 1656
Nicosia 162
tel +357 2 467 000
fax +357 2 476 613

Czech Republic
Richard Novak
Ernst & Young CS Consulting
Vinohradska 184
130 52 Prague 3
tel +42 2 6713 3010
fax +42 2 6713 30 12

Denmark
Allan Marker
Ernst & Young A/S
Tagensvej 86
DK-2200 Copenhagen N
tel +45 35 82 48 48
fax +45 35 82 48 00

Estonia
Kari Björk
Ernst & Young Esti AS
Tallinn Business Centre
Harju Street 6, 5th Floor
EE0001 Tallinn
tel +372 6 310 613
fax +372 6 310 611

Finland
Tomi Englund
Tilintarkastajien Oy
Oy Ernst & Young Ab
Kaivokatu 8
00100 Helsinki
tel +358 0 172 771
fax +358 0 622 1323

France
Jack Anderson
Ernst & Young
Tour Manhatten
Cedex 21
92095 Paris, La Défense 2
tel +33 1 46 93 70 00
fax +33 1 47 67 01 06

Germany
Anne Seidensticker
Ernst & Young
PO Box 102252
Am Wehrhahn 50, 40211 Dusseldorf
tel +49 211 93 52 0
fax +49 211 93 52 693

Gibraltar
Charles Serruya
Ernst & Young
Suite 5, International House
Bell Lane
PO Box 78
tel +350 79 799
fax +350 75 141

Greece
Themis Lianopoulos
Ernst & Young
Athens Tower A, Floor 23
2 Messogion Street
GR-115 27 Athens
tel +30 1 7759 780-4
fax +30 1 7759 790

Guernsey
Stephen Harlow
Ernst & Young
PO Box 236, 14 New Street
St Peter Port
Guernsey GY1 4LE
tel +44 1 481 723 232
fax +44 1 481 710 091

Hungary
Adam Tertak
Ernst & Young Kft
1146 Budapest
Hermina út 17
tel +36 1 252 8333
fax +36 1 251 8778

Ireland
Pat Talbot
Ernst & Young
Ernst & Young Building
Harcourt Centre
Harcourt Street
Dublin 2
tel +353 1 475 0555
fax +353 1 475 0599

Isle of Man
Paul Duffy
Ernst & Young
Derby House
Athol Street
Douglas
tel +44 624 6266 61
fax +44 624 626 375

Italy
Alastair Robertson
Reconta Ernst & Young
Via Torino 68
20123 Milan
tel +39 2 722 121
fax +39 2 722 120 37

Japan
Shigeru Fujita
Showa Ota & Co
Hibiya Kokusai Bldg
2-2-3 Uchisaiwai-cho
Chiyoda-ku
Tokyo 100
tel +81 3 3503 1191
fax +81 3 3503 1277

Jersey
John de Veulle
Ernst & Young
Le Gallais Chambers
54 Bath Street
St Helier
tel +44 1 534 501 000
fax +44 1 534 232 65

Kazakhstan
Johnathon Muir
Ernst & Young Kazakhstan
Almaty 48009
Prospect Abaya 153a
tel +7 3272 509 425
fax +7 3272 509 427

Korea
In Young Bong/Ken Cook
Young Wha Accounting Corporation
Dae Yu Building, Floors 11-14
25-15 Yeoido-dong
Youngdeungpo-ku, Seoul
tel +82 2 783 1100
fax +82 2 786 5890

Netherlands
Jan Siemons
Ernst & Young
PO Box 3101
Varrolaan 100
3584 BW Utrecht
tel +31 30 588 588
fax +31 30 588 100

Norway
Unne Vjelland
Ernst & Young
Stenersgaten 10
N-0184 Oslo
tel +47 22 86 27 00
fax +47 22 17 54 52

Poland
Derek Chrusciak
Ernst & Young
Ul Wspólna 62
00-684 Warsaw
tel +48 39 12 08 03
fax +48 22 29 42 63

Portugal
Luis Rosa
Ernst & Young
Apartado 1137
1003 Lisbon Codex
tel +351 1 352 88 89
fax +351 1 54 12 94

Russia
John Braden/Richard Lewis
Ernst & Young Vneshconsult
103062 Moscow
Podsoensky Pereulok 20/12
tel +7 502 220 46 87
fax +7 502 220 4682

Slovakia
Maria Praxl
Ernst & Young CS Consulting
Riecna 1
81513 Bratislava
tel +42 7 330 750
fax +42 901 700 258

Spain
Joaquin Velasco
Ernst & Young
Tor Picasso
Plaza Pablo Ruiz Picasso
28020 Madrid
tel +34 1572 7200
fax +34 1 572 7400

Sweden
Per Engstrom
Ernst & Young
Adolf Fredriks Kyrkogata 2
Box 3143
103 62 Stockholm
tel +46 8 613 90 00
fax +46 8 10 57 38

Switzerland
Jurg Scheller
Atag Ernst & Young
Belpstrasse 23
PO Box 5032
CH 3001 Berne
tel +41 31 320 61 11
fax +41 31 382 16 21

Turkey
H Alp Bayulken
Ernst & Young AS
Yildiz Posta Caddesi 26/16
Yesil Apartmani B Blok
80280 Esentepe
Istanbul
tel +90 212 274 9966
fax +90 212 274 9293

UK
David Rees/Barry Bright
Ernst & Young
Becket House
1 Lambeth Palace Road
London SE1 7EU
tel +44 171 928 2000
fax +44 171 928 1345

Ukraine
Tim Bloomfield
Ernst & Young Ukraina
Kiev 252053
Kiyanovsky Pereulok 3/7
tel +7 044 212 35 64
fax +7 044 212 5225

US
Barry Barovick/Richard Greene
Ernst & Young
1285 Avenue of the Americas
New York
NY 10019
tel +1 212 773 3000
fax +1 212 773 6350

The table below provides some key economic indicators of the countries covered by this edition of 'Regions of the New Europe'

	Population (million)	GDP (US$ billion)	Area ('000 sq km)	GDP per capita ('000 US$)	Population density (people per sq km)
Albania	3.4	1.1	28.7	0.3	118
Armenia	3.6	0.6	29.8	0.2	121
Austria	8.0	195.6	83.9	24.5	95
Belarus	10.3	n/a	207.6	n/a	50
Belgium	10.0	226.7	30.5	22.7	328
Bulgaria	8.5	8.7	110.9	1.0	77
Croatia	4.8	12.0	56.5	2.5	85
Czech Republic	10.5	30.8	78.9	2.9	133
Denmark	5.2	147.4	43.1	28.3	121
Estonia	1.6	1.8	45.1	1.1	35
Finland	5.1	95.9	337.1	18.8	15
France	57.7	1,318.9	544.0	22.9	106
Germany	81.2	2,041.5	356.9	25.1	228
Greece	10.4	77.6	132.0	7.5	79
Hungary	10.5	34.8	93.0	3.3	113
Ireland	3.6	51.8	70.3	14.4	51
Italy	57.1	1,020.2	301.3	17.9	190
Latvia	2.7	2.4	64.5	0.9	42
Lithuania	3.8	2.8	65.3	1.4	58
Luxembourg	0.4	13.8	2.6	34.0	154
Macedonia	1.9	n/a	25.7	n/a	75
Moldova	4.4	n/a	33.7	n/a	131
Netherlands	15.3	328.5	41.2	21.5	371
Norway	4.3	108.2	323.9	25.2	13
Poland	38.6	72.9	312.7	1.9	123
Portugal	9.9	87.5	92.4	8.8	107
Romania	23.4	15.5	237.5	0.7	99
Russia	149.5	130.2	17,075.4	0.9	9
Slovakia	5.3	10.9	49.0	2.1	108
Slovenia	2.0	10.7	20.3	5.4	99
Spain	39.1	480.3	504.8	12.3	77
Sweden	8.7	194.7	450.0	22.4	19
Switzerland	6.9	259.6	41.3	37.6	167
Turkey	59.5	134.5	779.5	2.3	76
Ukraine	52.3	24.8	603.7	0.5	87
UK	57.8	1,013.6	244.1	17.5	237

Source: OECD and EBRD, various publications, 1995

Chapter 1

INTRODUCTION, OVERVIEW AND LISTINGS

The image many people have of Europe is of a predictable, reasonably wealthy and stable region, if not a dynamic one. How wrong can they be? The last decade has seen some of the biggest changes in the European map since the end of the Second World War. The break-up of the former USSR and Yugoslavia has seen the spawning of more than 10 new European countries. The European Union has attracted three new members and more are knocking on the door to join. We have witnessed the reunification of Germany and the disunion of the Czech and Slovak republics. Civil war continues in parts of the former Yugoslavia as well as in Russia and a number of former Soviet republics. Communism has been overthrown only to see ex-communists being elected to positions of power in former communist states. Germany has experienced a worse strike record than the United Kingdom and suffered a decline in output for the first time in many years. Unemployment in the West remains stubbornly high while the fastest growing economy in the region is that of Turkey.

Many companies have taken their eyes off the 'dull' European market, attracted instead to the booming economies of Asia. But Europe can still offer a marketplace of 800 million people in an area smaller than North America. Despite moves towards a single European market, a single currency and general harmonisation, it remains one of the most diverse cultural and economic regions of the world. Most of the world's estimated 40,000 multinational enterprises have some form of operation established within the region (according to the UN Programme on Transnational Corporations). The vast majority of these multinationals come from three regions – North America, South East Asia and Europe itself – with approximately two-thirds of them in the service sector and one-third in manufacturing.

The road from being a domestic company to becoming a transnational and eventually global company can take many different routes. In general, however, companies tend to establish operations in a new country for one of the following main reasons:
● Better access to customers in that country/region/market provides improved service levels, offsets the cost of exporting to that location, or avoids trade barriers. For example, in the past a number of Japanese firms established manufacturing operations in the European Union to avoid anti-dumping and quota barriers; similarly, Western European companies are now establishing manufacturing plants in Eastern Europe in order to avoid high tariff barriers on exported goods to the latter region;
● To reduce operating costs. There are many examples of German companies 'border hopping', that is, moving manufacturing production into France or Central/Eastern Europe in order to reduce operating costs by using lower-cost labour. In an attempt to reduce costs, however, some firms have moved operations out of Europe altogether. For example, a number of Europe-based companies have moved their data-processing and billing activities to the Indian subcontinent.

The main modes of cross-border investment are:
● Greenfield;
● Mergers and acquisition;
● Joint ventures.

There are around 1,000 cross-border greenfield investments in Europe in any particular year (excluding the establishment of sales offices and new branches of foreign banks and other similar service activities, which tend to serve a national rather than an international market). Within this total there are many where there has been little real choice of country. For example, a bottling plant serving the Polish market is almost certain to be built in Poland, while the requirement to have a component factory within 30 minutes' drive-time of, say, an automotive assembly plant greatly limits the location choice. The figure of 1,000 investments does not, however, take into account the large amount of new intra-country investments, which are of interest to regional agencies, nor the many expansion and follow-on investment decisions that are made each year.

These follow-on investments are of two different kinds: either a company is deciding where to create a new production line for a new product (this is just as much a location decision as the establishment of a greenfield operation); or, as the company becomes increasingly global but its resources remain limited, it has to choose whether to develop product A in region X or product B in region Y – again, the decision-making process is similar to that of a site selection.

We are also witnessing an increasing degree of rationalisation of established companies operating within Europe. Often the outcome is not a new location – frequently, in fact, the result is a consolidation to fewer or just one site – but there are exceptions. These moves to rationalise/consolidate are driven by the need to view Europe as a single market rather than separate national markets. This represents an important new dimension to the overall inward investment marketplace. For companies, establishing the optimal location configuration demands a similar set of decision-making processes as a new investment, while for agencies it means competing to retain and build on existing investments.

In the past, companies seeking assistance with mergers, acquisitions and joint ventures have turned to their financial advisers, accountants, lawyers and merchant banks. As agencies realise the sheer volume of such activity and witness at best zero growth in greenfield investments – at worst a decline – more of them are looking to provide this kind of assistance in an attempt to attract investments to their locality.

In part due to high unemployment and the need to restructure local and national economies, an ever-growing number of agencies are attempting to attract inward investment into their region. There are probably more than 1,000 such organisations in Europe which have as their sole or a key objective the attraction of inward investment. The huge level of competition between these agencies increases the complexity of the location decision-making process, as hundreds of towns and regions try to convince companies that theirs is the best location in which to establish a new European operation.

What companies need to recognise is that there is no single best location in Europe for an investment. Rather, each country and each region has certain competitive advantages which make it attractive to certain types of investment.

This third edition of *Regions of the New Europe* compares the regions and countries of Europe in terms of the main location factors companies take into account when making a site-selection decision. In addition, we have included this year an overview of inward investment trends in Europe and an assessment of the way in which companies make location decisions. As with previous editions, we have also set out our view about potential European locations for particular types of projects.

Inward investment trends

The opening up of Central and Eastern Europe and the recent votes on European Union (EU) membership have had a major impact on flows of foreign direct investment. Ernst & Young's latest surveys of outward investment from the US (the major source of inward investment into Europe) have found that 20 per cent of investments into Europe are going to the former communist Eastern bloc countries. We are also seeing companies in Norway and Switzerland considering moving operations into EU countries, following their electorates' rejection of the European Union and European Economic Area (EEA) respectively. In Germany and Belgium, meanwhile, high operating costs continue to force companies to reconsider their locations and relocate to lower-cost countries.

Europe is likely to experience increased competition for inward investment projects from Mediterranean countries such as Tunisia, Israel, Palestine, and the fastest growing economy in the region, Turkey. In the longer term, as the economies of Eastern and Southern Europe further develop, investments will start to flow westwards, while the increasing internationalisation of companies based in the Indian subcontinent and in Latin America will lead to a growth in investment into Europe from these regions too, albeit at relatively low levels. For the foreseeable future, however, we believe that North America will continue to be the main source of inward investment in Europe.

Other trends that have been witnessed are changes in companies' operating procedures and the nature of projects. There is an increased move towards global products assembled in low-cost locations – often outside Europe – with packaging and finishing being carried out closer to the customer, thereby continuing the rationalisation of manufacturing while localising customer services and support. On the other hand, new technologies enable the move from mass production to mass customisation, that is, making a wide range of products on short production runs in smaller factories. This trend could lead to a move back to local production for local consumption.

Generally, technology is having significant and increasing effects both on manufacturing and on services locations. In manufacturing, companies are adopting more integrated approaches to supply-chain management; these place stringent performance demands on suppliers, and in many cases on their locations as well. For example, the requirements of just-in-time (JIT) manufacturing have a significant impact on suppliers.

In services, the key driver of change is the growth in the use of intelligent telecommunications networks whereby many operations can be located further from customers. This is happening at a pan-European level, with the advent of SSCs (Shared Service Centres) for multinationals, and an increase in call centres operating on a multinational, multilingual basis.

Another major change is in the mode of foreign investment. Most large companies from South East Asia and North America are already established in Europe. For smaller companies, opening a new facility in a different continent is a major risk. There is therefore greater interest in joint ventures and licence agreements. Moreover, as product life-cycles decrease and as research and development costs rise, companies are increasingly keen to work together to bring new products to the marketplace. Aerospace and electronics are examples of sectors where this is occurring increasingly. This kind of globalisation and partnership means that there is often less need to establish new facilities in a new location.

With all these changes taking place, how important is inward investment to Europe? The answer is given by a few statistics relating to Japanese investment in the region. According to the Japanese External Trade Relations Office, there are fewer than 800 Japanese manufacturing plants in Europe. However, they:
● Employ approximately 220,000 people;
● Achieve sales of around $50 billion a year.

Perhaps of greater significance is the fact that 75 per cent of these plants have been established for less than 10 years. (These figures exclude the enormous impact in terms of job creation on local suppliers.) Given the impact of such investment in a region, it is not surprising there is so much competition to attract inward investment.

A new location: the decision-making process

No two companies make a location decision in the same way. Each decision is unique, taking into account the company's:
● Product;
● Size;
● Customer and supply base;
● Aspirations and long-term strategy;
● Type of activity (office, production, distribution);
● The degree and scope of competition.

Companies need to recognise that there is no single best location for an investment: each country and each region has certain competitive advantages

There are probably over 1,000 organisations in Europe which have as their sole or key objective the attraction of inward investment

10

Nonetheless, there are factors which are common to most location decisions to a lesser or greater extent. These are touched on below and in greater detail within the main body of this book.

The political and economic picture

Most companies have tended to take political stability in Europe for granted. Sadly, this is not the case. Civil war in Bosnia may be an extreme example of instability but it is not the only one. Further east, internal disputes within Russia continue to cause concern, with various territories demanding independence while political in-fighting over who should run the country rumbles on. Sky-high inflation and general political instability also continue to hinder moves towards economic reform and higher living standards.

But it is not just in the East that there are problems: Italy continues to stumble from crisis to crisis with an average of a new government every year; investigations into organised crime and corruption seem to have caught every Italian institution in their net. The reasonably amicable divorce of the Czech and Slovak republics could still prove to be a precedent for Belgium, which is moving rapidly towards a fully federal state. Meanwhile Norway and Switzerland are in danger of becoming increasingly isolated outside the European Union, though being non-members does offer them some offsetting advantages. On the economic front it is the economies of Eastern Europe that are likely to be the engines of growth, with a rapid increase in output forecast for Poland, the Czech Republic, Hungary and, further east, Turkey.

Labour issues

There are many labour issues that companies need to consider before making a location decision. As well as costs and availability, these include skill levels, hire-and-fire legislation, working hours restrictions, the scope of collective agreements and their binding nature as well as attitudes to work, flexibility and overall productivity.

Labour costs include not only the wages paid to individuals but also all the statutory and customary add-ons such as social security and pension contributions. There is an increasing realisation among governments that countries with low levels of these add-ons – for example Denmark, Ireland and the UK – have a major advantage over competing nations. There has therefore been a move to try to reduce the burden of such add-on costs. The scope for achieving this is often limited, as governments are also grappling with ways of reducing budget deficits. Eastern and Southern Europe have by far the lowest labour costs in Europe. However, even the lowest cost countries in Europe are considerably undercut by parts of Asia. This underlines the fact that Europe cannot compete on cost alone, but must do so on the basis of higher productivity, service, quality and strategic differentiation.

As companies within Europe move their labour-intensive activities to regions with low labour costs, and as transnational works councils gain more power, there is likely to be some convergence in wage levels. This is likely to be a very slow process, and wide disparities will remain for a considerable time.

As the use of technology increases, the skills required by business continue to evolve. And as workplaces are delayered, there is a greater demand for inter-personal skills and a willingness to take decisions and take responsibility. While business skills are still lacking in many Eastern European countries, there remains a highly skilled workforce with world-leading scientists and engineers. One problem facing East European countries is a brain drain, with the best people leaving for the US. There have, however, been moves in the opposite direction, such as AT&T Bell Laboratories' contract with the Institute of General Physics of the Russian Academy of Sciences, currently involved in the design of a fibre-optic telephone network.

One factor that companies often pay great attention to in making a site selection is the level of unionisation and strikes. This throws up some interesting information, such as the fact that the density of union membership in Switzerland is over twice that of Spain, whereas the level of days lost due to disputes is over 500 times higher in the latter. In countries where binding collective agreements are in force, membership of trade unions is often seen as unnecessary. In France, for example, only some 10 per cent of the workforce are unionised, but over 90 per cent are covered by collective bargaining agreements.

Two opposing arguments about employment legislation are currently being advanced in Europe. The first is that we must ensure the highest common level of worker protection across Europe to avoid the issue of 'social dumping' – that is, companies being attracted to locations with more relaxed employment legislation than elsewhere, or bringing in non-national employees who will work for poorer pay and conditions. This line is strongly supported by Germany, which has seen an outflow of work to countries with lower labour costs and more relaxed labour regimes. The other view, taken mainly by the UK, is that in order to ensure Europe remains competitive, there should be as few restrictions as possible, and pay and conditions should be set by the marketplace – hence the abolition in the UK of a minimum wage. How these arguments will develop in the future is difficult to foresee, but increasing pressure on Western European labour markets as they are undercut by those in the East is likely to result in increased tension.

Market accessibility: a key factor

The ability to get a product to the marketplace is *the* key location factor. The two main issues are:
● The physical movement of goods, services and people;
● The legal movement of goods and services.

The first is a combination of distance from the market and availability of suitable infrastructure. Vast amounts of resources have gone into improving transport infrastructure, especially between East and West. At present, the regions with the greatest market access are those in the so-called 'hot banana' running from the south east of England, through the Benelux countries, the Ruhr in Germany, on to Switzerland and northern Italy. But with the economies of the East forecast to grow faster than those in the West, this is likely to change. Regions in the Czech Republic, Hungary and eastern Germany will begin to gain, probably at the expense of those in south west France, Spain and parts of Scandinavia.

As the use of technology increases, the skills required by business continue to evolve

11

Something which makes a mockery of moves to improve physical access between East and West is the imposition of trade barriers by the European Union on products from the former communist countries. Steps have been taken to reduce the extent of such barriers but their retention will slow the rate of economic growth in both regions. Another major barrier to trade in Eastern Europe is the long border delays being experienced at many points of entry into the European Union and between countries such as the Ukraine and Poland. These delays can run into days and are likely to worsen with the new Schengen agreement, which allows open borders within most of the European Union, but more stringent external borders.

Property: a question of supply and demand

Like most goods in a free market, the price of property is dependent on supply and demand. Excess supply in most Western cities in the last few years has resulted in a collapse in rental prices, while the shortage of suitable office space in many Eastern European cities has led to soaring rental levels, with firms often finding it cheaper to do business out of hotel bedrooms.

What is the future for office space? Significant amounts of office space are rapidly becoming outdated because the information superhighway demands different layouts and design. Environmental considerations, meanwhile, have led to the development of energy-efficient buildings which can mean savings in running costs.

As companies continue to seek ways of reducing costs, the office is a prime candidate for review. Rarely fully utilised, it can be an inefficient resource. In the short term, companies are reducing the amount of space they take through means such as hotelling, 'hot-desking' and holding information on disk and CD-ROM rather than in paper files. The move to teleworking raises the question of whether many of the large offices of today will be needed at all in future.

In the case of industrial space, a number of authorities are currently reviewing the importance of ensuring an adequate supply of speculative space. While it is beneficial to have suitable premises available for immediate occupation, their provision can be expensive. An alternative is a rapid turnaround of planning permission and the use of fast-build techniques.

Communications and transport

Both physical and electronic communications are key drivers for many companies. Advances in telecommunications continue at a frantic pace. Increasing liberalisation and the globalisation of service providers mean increased competition, better services and faster innovation. Within Europe, the UK has probably the most liberalised market, which has led to some of the cheapest telecom services. However, over the next few years most other European countries will close the gap as they liberalise their markets. A drawback of a too-liberalised market is that incompatible systems can be installed – a problem that has arisen in Russia. Another dilemma in the former communist countries is the poor state of the infrastructure and waiting lists for new connections which run into many years.

With physical transport, the great paradox is that rising demand is coupled with massive losses by the main service providers, be they airlines, railways or barge companies. Infrastructure demand far outstripping supply remains the main problem for both land and air transport, and rising congestion leads to companies incurring additional costs. In manufacturing, for example, to ensure that customer demand for just-in-time deliveries is met, companies often have to establish local distribution and warehouse centres rather than delivering direct from the factory. (As for video-conferencing, although its increased use may reduce business travel, its impact is likely to remain minor for the foreseeable future.)

The rise in congestion has occurred mainly in central regions, making many more peripheral locations an attractive proposition for international companies in a wide range of sectors provided there are reasonable regional airport and motorway links. On the other hand, increasing congestion may have a different effect on the location of business: to ensure just-in-time production, companies often require component suppliers to co-locate with them, or at least within very short drive-times. This can in turn lead to a concentration of manufacturing, reversing a long-running trend to decentralise.

At present, transport infrastructure is best developed in the Benelux countries, the Rhine-Ruhr region of Germany, the Ile de France and the south east of England (though these also tend to be the most congested regions). In Eastern Europe, the infrastructure is grossly inadequate to meet the demands placed on it. In Poland, for example, it is estimated that $50 billion of investment is needed to bring the transport infrastructure up to the required level. Given the shortage of resources, many Eastern European countries have turned to the private sector to build and charge for the use of much-needed road links; privatisation is also proposed or has been undertaken at ports, airlines and railways.

Meeting energy needs

The reliance of many European countries on imports to meet their energy needs is a cause for some concern, prompting France, for example, to develop its nuclear industry to maximise its security of supply. This concern has led to a reluctance in many countries to liberalise energy markets, with the result that electricity and gas prices in Europe are generally far in excess of those in the US. In the long term, many European nations will be reliant on just two countries within Europe for their gas supplies – Russia and Norway. As a result, a number of joint ventures have been set up by European gas companies to investigate the possibility of building gas pipelines from the Middle East and North Africa to increase the number of sources of supply. (This would also help Turkey and Greece and other Balkan states to extend their present small natural gas networks.)

In the case of electricity, the main concern is the need to replace Eastern Europe's outdated generating capacity – especially its nuclear capacity – and to clean up emissions from Poland's coal-burning plants.

The environment: an increasingly important issue

As already mentioned, the environment now plays an increasingly important role in a company's decisions. Although the rise of 'green' or

The shortage of suitable office space in many Eastern European cities has led to soaring rental levels

environmental political parties came to a halt during the Europe-wide recession of the early 1990s, and there was a backlash against green policies in the Netherlands after recent flooding, environmental issues have undoubtedly entered the mainstream political arena.

While the enforcement of environmental laws varies from region to region, the potential negative consumer reaction to perceived poor environmental standards has led many to consider seriously environmental issues in their location decision-making. For example, chemical companies, which often have a negative environmental image, now actively avoid locations with a poor environmental reputation as this reinforces the image of the sector. Instead they see an advantage in being located in regions with high environmental standards, even if this means increased operating costs. The general view is that environmental standards will become more strict in future, so it is better to ensure that any new plant meets the highest possible standards now, rather than having to upgrade facilities at great expense in years to come. Regions selling themselves on the basis of relaxed enforcement of environmental legislation may soon find their approach counterproductive. Measures are now being introduced to deal with contaminated land which will impose additional burdens on companies and may result in greater pressure to develop greenfield sites.

Financial incentives and taxation

The ability to offer financial incentives often helps regions to get on a company's shortlist of locations. However, shortages of resources mean that many Southern and Eastern European countries are unable to offer significant levels of support. In these regions, tax incentives – either reduced tax rates or tax-free periods – become more important. From a company's perspective it should be remembered that grants are generally one-offs and tax breaks are temporary. What is more important is whether the location is going to be profitable in the long term.

As we have said, there is considerable competition to attract new foreign investment; even in regions that are unable to offer grants against capital expenditure or for job creation, there is usually some way in which the local authorities can provide assistance, whether in cash or in kind. This might take the form of assistance with recruitment and training, planning and operating permits, introductions to possible suppliers or servicing the site.

The expatriate workforce

The free movement of goods and people allowed by the Single European Market and the opening up of new markets in the former communist bloc has led to large numbers of individuals working in foreign countries as expatriates. This trend is likely to persist as companies continue to internationalise and as a pan-European job market evolves. Offsetting this trend is companies' desire to reduce the huge expense of employing expatriates. In Eastern Europe there is a growing demand to employ local managers or returned émigrés rather than expensive expatriates who often do not have the right mix of language and business skills. In Western Europe, improved telecommunications have led to a move towards virtual company structures, thus a manager in London can report to a director in Paris while being responsible for staff in Brussels and Rotterdam. This type of structure means that staff can change jobs and gain promotion without having to move from their home office, thereby greatly reducing relocation expenses. Those staff who do move between countries are increasingly being employed on local terms and conditions, again avoiding expensive expatriate benefits such as housing and schooling.

Overview and listings

We have shown that there is a very wide variety of factors which impact on location decisions. Factors vary in importance according to:
- Sector;
- Project type;
- Country of origin;
- Company considerations.

There is no single (or simple) answer to the question 'Which is the best location in Europe for an internationally mobile investment?' For many projects there is a trade-off between the advantages of being located in Europe's economic centre – say, parts of Germany, France, Switzerland or the Benelux countries – and the benefits of lower operating costs which are usually to be found in the more peripheral regions such as the Iberian Peninsula, Greece, Ireland and Eastern Europe. Much of France, Italy and the UK is in an intermediate position in terms both of proximity to the economic centre and operating costs, which are generally higher than in the peripheral regions but lower than in the Benelux countries and Western Germany.

To demonstrate how the optimum location depends on the circumstances of the project in question, we have prepared listings of possible locations for a number of hypothetical projects for non-European companies. These listings bring together the various detailed location factors discussed in the body of the report. The weights we have applied to particular factors in each listing are intended to reflect our experience of the general importance of those factors to specific types of project. However, it must be stressed that the exercise should be regarded as illustrative only, indicating some of the regions worthy of consideration for particular types of projects. Excluded regions could easily prove to be the most appropriate location for similar projects, once account is taken of the individual circumstances of the company and its project. There is, in fact, often little to choose between regions within and outside the rankings, especially if the regions are in the same country. We must emphasise that for particular client projects we have recommended locations outside the listings, as well as locations included in the listings.

Apart from eastern Germany, we have not included former communist bloc countries within the main listings. (However information on some of these countries is included in later chapters; we fully recognise that many regions in the former communist bloc are now considered alongside regions in Western Europe when companies make their location decisions.) Instead, we provide a separate listing of investment opportunities in Central and Eastern Europe, taking into account political as well as economic factors.

The ability to offer financial incentives often helps regions to get on a company's shortlist of locations

Grants are generally one-offs: what is more important is whether the location is going to be profitable in the long term

13

This listing is given at the end of the chapter. In each case regions are listed in *alphabetical order*.

Electronics/telecoms equipment (manufacturing)

Companies are assumed to be looking for a skilled labour force with some experience in the sector, labour availability, a competitive cost structure and in many cases some financial incentives.

Bavaria, Germany
Denmark
East France
East Spain
Finland
Ireland
Lombardy, Italy
North England, UK
North Rhine Westphalia, Germany
Northern Ireland, UK
Scotland, UK
South West France
Wales, UK
West France
West Netherlands

Automotives (including components and related industries)

Proximity to markets and good transport links, industrial traditions including labour force flexibility, cost competitiveness and some financial incentives are often important location factors.

Bavaria, Germany
East France
East Midlands, UK
East Spain
Flanders, Belgium
West Sweden
Lombardy, Italy
Nord-Pas-de-Calais, France
North England, UK
North East Spain
North West Italy
Saarland, Germany
South Netherlands
Thuringia, Germany
Wales, UK
West Midlands, UK
West France

Chemicals, including speciality chemicals

Industrial tradition (including willingness to work shifts, labour regulations), good transport links, environmental considerations and financial incentives are among the relevant location factors.

East Spain
East France
Flanders, Belgium
Lower Saxony, Germany
Mediterranean France
Nord-Pas-de-Calais, France
North England, UK
North Netherlands
North West Italy
North West England, UK
South Netherlands
South West France
North West and Berne, Switzerland
Wallonia, Belgium
Yorkshire and Humberside, UK

Basic assembly

For a company seeking a greenfield site for a medium to large-sized general manufacturing or assembly facility, the factors to be taken into account may include: labour availability, cost and regulations; proximity to markets and the quality of transport infrastructure; and the possible availability of incentives. Southern Europe with its low labour costs, and the UK with its relatively low labour costs and relaxed labour regulations, are well represented.

Abruzzi Molise, Italy
Central Greece
Centre East, France
East Spain
Flanders, Belgium
Ireland
Nord-Pas-de-Calais, France
North East Spain
North Portugal
North England, UK
Northern Ireland
Saxony, Germany
Scotland, UK
South Netherlands
Thrace, Turkey
Wales, UK
West Midlands, UK

Research and development centre

Emphasis is given to the size and quality of the R&D sector, skill levels, reasonable international transport and telecommunication links, and a relatively central location.

Bavaria, Germany
Centre East, France
Denmark
East Anglia, UK
Flanders, Belgium
Ile de France, France
Lombardy, Italy
Mediterranean France
North Rhine Westphalia, Germany
Scotland, UK
South East UK
Stockholm, Sweden
North East Switzerland
Vienna, Austria
Wallonia, Belgium
West Netherlands

European regional headquarters

Key location factors include excellent international transport links; a well-educated labour force; attractive location for international executives; labour costs; favourable corporate and expatriate taxation; good telecommunications.

Berlin, Germany
Brussels, Belgium
Denmark
Flanders, Belgium
Hamburg, Germany
Hessen, Germany
Ile de France, France
Lombardy, Italy
Luxembourg, Luxembourg
Madrid, Spain
North Rhine Westphalia, Germany
North East Switzerland
South East UK
South Netherlands
Wallonia, Belgium
Vienna, Austria
West Netherlands
West Switzerland

Exhibit 1.1: Rankings for Central and Eastern European countries (1 = best rating, 5 = worst rating)							
	Business opportunities	Political risk	Credit rating	Status of local economy	Stability	Business infrastructure	Total
Czech Republic	2	1	1	3	1	2	10
Poland	1	2	2	3	2	2	12
Hungary	3	2	2	3	2	2	14
Slovenia	4	2	2	3	2	2	15
Estonia	4	2	3	3	2	2	16
Latvia	4	2	3	3	2	3	17
Lithuania	4	2	3	3	2	4	18
Bulgaria	3	3	4	3	3	3	19
Kazakhstan	2	3	3	4	3	4	19
Romania	2	3	4	3	3	4	19
Russia	1	4	4	3	5	3	20
Slovakia	4	3	3	4	3	3	20
Belarus	3	3	4	4	3	4	21
Uzbekistan	3	4	3	4	3	4	21
Ukraine	2	4	5	4	4	3	22
Croatia	4	4	4	4	3	4	23
Albania	4	4	4	4	4	4	24
Kyrgyz Republic	4	4	4	4	4	4	24
Moldova	4	4	4	4	4	4	24
Armenia	4	4	5	4	4	5	26
Azerbaijan	3	5	4	5	5	4	26
Turkmenistan	5	4	5	5	4	4	27
Georgia	5	4	5	5	4	5	28
Former Yugoslavia*	5	5	5	5	5	5	30
Macedonia*	5	5	5	5	5	5	30
Tadzhikistan	5	5	5	5	5	5	30

* Former Yugoslavia – until the cessation of hostilities, we are not commenting on the status for investment in Yugoslavia and Macedonia.

Source: *Ernst & Young Emerging Markets Profiles*, April 1995. Countries are rated on the basis of inward investors' perception of the emerging markets, based on the following categories:
● Business opportunities = size and structure of domestic market and attitudes towards foreign investment ● Political risk = stability of government and market-oriented policies
● Credit rating = external debt and attitude of international financial markets ● Status of local economy = domestic economic performance ● Stability = overall political and economic stability ● Business infrastructure = legal framework, professional services, telecommunications and distribution.

European distribution centre

Key considerations for this kind of project include proximity to main European markets, very good transport infrastructure and property costs. Not surprisingly, regions at the centre of the EEA dominate.

Baden Württemberg, Germany
East Netherlands
East France
Flanders, Belgium
Hamburg, Germany
Hessen, Germany
Nord-Pas-de-Calais, France
North Rhine Westphalia, Germany
South Netherlands
Wallonia, Belgium
West Netherlands
Paris Basin, France
South East UK

Telecommunications call centres

Handling both incoming and outgoing calls, key requirements are cost/quality of telecom services, and availability and cost of multilingual staff.

Brussels, Belgium
Denmark
East Netherlands
Flanders, Belgium
Ireland
North Netherlands
South Netherlands
East France
West Netherlands
South East UK
Stockholm, Sweden
Centre East, France
Norway

The Czech Republic, Poland, Hungary and now also Slovenia have made significant strides towards establishing a working market economy

Central/Eastern European country rankings

Exhibit 1.1 (above) ranks the countries of Central and Eastern Europe. Drawn from the quarterly assessment of emerging markets prepared by Ernst & Young, these rankings reflect our assessment of the relative attractiveness of these countries according to a number of different criteria. Our assessment is based on sources of data from both within and outside Ernst & Young.

The rankings continue to show that the countries of Central and Eastern Europe fall into three broad divisions. In the first division, countries such as the Czech Republic, Poland, Hungary and probably now also Slovenia have made significant strides towards establishing a working market economy. This is reflected in their success in attracting foreign direct investment.

The second group, which consists of countries as different as Russia, Slovakia, the Baltic states, Romania and Bulgaria, represents those economies that are only now beginning to register as genuine world emerging markets and which still have some way to go. The reasons for the inclusion of these countries in this group vary. In the case of Russia, for example, political risk is still the dominant factor; in Romania and Bulgaria, by way of contrast, the reforms process is only now getting under way.

The third group consists of those countries at the beginning of their reform process. It includes many of the Central Asian states and other countries within the former Soviet Union. The attractiveness of these countries for foreign direct investment is largely influenced by whether natural resources such as oil and gas are located within their borders.

Chapter 2

INWARD INVESTMENT TRENDS

Foreign investment activity, whether by direct investment or strategic alliance, is recovering after the worldwide recession of the early 1990s as companies continue to internationalise their operations, facilitated by the liberalisation of the world economies. At the same time, an ever-growing number of governments at both national and local level are striving to attract new foreign investment and retain or expand existing operations.

Estimates of foreign investment flows are provided by national governments and international organisations such as the United Nations (UN), the Organisation for Economic Co-operation and Development (OECD) and the European Union (EU). However, differences in definitions and in the comprehensiveness of data make cross-country comparisons difficult. Information on 'projects' is even more problematic, as there is no standard definition. Drawing on a wide range of international and government sources, private surveys and development agency reports, this chapter provides a brief overview of the main trends in foreign direct investment (FDI) and concludes with an analysis of their implications for those seeking to attract inward investment projects. The main topics covered are:

● Global investment trends;
● Origin of FDI into Europe;
● Destination of FDI into Europe;
● Mode of FDI;
● Sector of FDI;
● Prospects for FDI –
in the 1990s,
in 2000 and beyond;
● The future for inward investment.

Investment trends: the global picture

The stock of global FDI is estimated to be in the region of US$2 trillion, concentrated in North America and Europe. As Exhibit 2.1 (below)

The stock of global FDI has shown signs of recovery, with annual flows increasing in 1993 for the first time since 1990

illustrates, flows of FDI increased significantly between 1985 and 1989, and peaked in 1990 before declining rapidly to 1992 (largely due to a decline in investment from Japan and, to a lesser degree, from Western Europe). More recently, FDI has shown signs of recovery, with annual flows increasing in 1993 for the first time since 1990.

According to the UN, there are now at least 37,000 multinational companies, with 170,000 foreign affiliates, the vast majority of which are based in OECD countries.

This renewed growth incorporates the the re-emergence of trends prevalent in the mid-1980s, with the United States, France and the United Kingdom again dominant as sources of outward FDI. Flows of FDI from Germany and Japan have not yet recovered to their previous levels, though their decline has slowed.

The United States, France and the United Kingdom are again dominant as sources of outward FDI

Exhibit 2.2: FDI flows, 1992

	Inflow % of world total	Outflow % of world total
Developed nations	**64.5**	**94.6**
(of which)		
EU	49.7	56.4
Others, Western Europe	2.3	5.3
North America	7.1	22.7
Others	5.6	10.3
Developing nations	**32.5**	**5.4**
(of which)		
Africa	1.9	0.1
Latin America/Caribbean	11.2	0.2
Developing Europe	0.1	–
Western Asia	0.5	0.3
E, S, SE Asia	18.6	4.8
Pacific	0.3	–
Central and Eastern Europe	2.8	0.1
All	**100**	**100**

Figures may not add up to 100 due to rounding.
Source: UN *World Investment Report* 1994

The most significant development in recent years has been the emergence of the developing nations as major recipients of FDI, accounting for a third of inflows. A dozen countries in Latin America and South East Asia receive the vast majority of this investment, with China being the star performer.

An additional new phenomenon is the growth of intra-South East Asian FDI, as the more developed countries, such as Korea, Singapore and Taiwan, attempt to increase the skill and value-added base of their economies, and as they begin to lose labour-intensive operations to China and Vietnam.

In contrast, FDI into the former communist countries of Europe has not been as significant as

Exhibit 2.1: Direct investment abroad from OECD countries – outflows

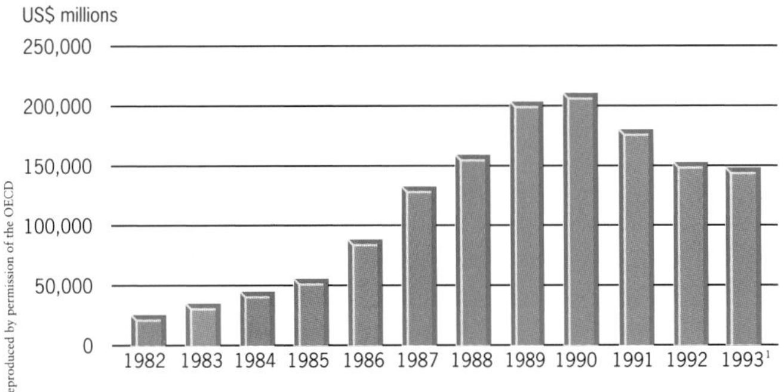

US$ millions

(1) Data for some major source countries of FDI such as Switzerland not yet available. Source: OECD *Financial Market Trends* 1994

Exhibit 2.3: Major new greenfield foreign investments in Europe in 1994

Company	Origin	Capital (US$ m)	Jobs	Location
Boston Scientific	US	32	500	Ireland
Daewoo	South Korea	110	n/a	France
Hualon Corp	Taiwan	220	1,800	UK
Mercedes/Swatch	Germany/Switzerland	500	1,950	France
Nippon Electric Glass/ Schutt Glasswerke	Japan/Germany	300	750	UK
Omega Engineering	US	35	500	UK
Samsung	South Korea	900	900-3,000	UK
Sensormatic	US	21	870	Ireland

Source: Ernst & Young/press announcements

Exhibit 2.4: Flows of direct foreign investment into the European Union

% FDI into the EU — US, Japan, Intra-EU

Source: Ernst & Young/OECD *International Direct Investment Statistics Yearbook* 1994

Exhibit 2.5: Inward investment flows into European countries, 1990-92

Location	1990 US$ m	1991 US$ m	1992 US$ m
European Union			
Austria	653	360	947
Belgium/Luxembourg	8,056	9,377	11,073
Denmark	1,132	1,553	1,073
Finland	812	(233)	387
France	13,223	15,149	21,843
Germany	8,390	7,390	6,800
Greece	1,005	1,135	1,144
Ireland	n/a	n/a	n/a
Italy	6,441	2,403	3,072
Netherlands	11,544	5,801	5,638
Portugal	2,610	2,448	1,873
Spain	13,841	10,502	8,058
Sweden	1,972	5,751	329
UK	32,669	16,158	18,182
Rest of Europe			
Bulgaria	4	56	42
Estonia	–	–	58
Former Czechoslovakia	207	600	1,103
Hungary	–	1,462	1,479
Latvia	–	–	14
Lithuania	–	–	10
Norway	1,003	(439)	897
Poland	89	291	678
Romania	–	40	77
Russian Federation	–	–	700
Switzerland	4,961	3,178	1,033

Source: UN *World Investment Report* 1994 (brackets imply disinvestment in a country)

expected or hoped for, following the region's transition to a market economy. For example, total flows of FDI into the region were only 40 per cent of those into China in 1992, and investments have so far been concentrated in just a few countries and sectors. However, in some sectors – for instance automotives and food and drink – there have been significant investments in Central European countries such as Poland. Moreover, future investments are likely to continue at a fairly constant rate in the most stable economies.

Exhibit 2.6: Japanese manufacturing plants in Europe

	Total	UK	France	Germany	Spain	Italy	Neth	Belgium	Ireland	Austria	Portugal	Sweden	Switz	Finland	Denmark	Greece	Lux	Norway
Total	728	206	121	106	64	52	45	40	31	17	12	10	8	5	3	3	3	1
Foods	33	4	21	3	1	–	3	1	–	–	–	–	–	–	–	–	–	–
Textile	16	4	2	1	1	3	–	–	2	1	2	–	–	–	–	–	–	–
Apparel and textile products	18	4	3	1	1	9	–	–	–	–	–	–	–	–	–	–	–	–
Furniture and equipment	6	2	2	–	1	–	1	–	–	–	–	–	–	2	–	–	–	–
Pulp and paper	5	–	–	1	1	–	–	–	–	–	1	–	–	–	–	–	–	–
Chemical	124	33	17	11	13	7	13	14	4	2	2	2	3	–	1	1	1	–
Pharmaceuticals	18	–	3	5	4	1	1	1	3	–	–	–	–	1	–	–	–	–
Rubber products	13	2	4	2	1	1	1	1	–	–	–	–	–	–	–	–	–	–
Ceramics, stone and clay	20	3	3	3	2	1	1	5	2	–	–	–	–	–	–	–	–	–
Iron and steel	4	–	–	1	1	–	1	–	–	–	–	–	–	–	1	–	–	–
Non-ferrous metals	14	4	4	1	–	1	–	–	2	–	1	–	–	–	–	–	–	–
Metal products	35	11	3	6	4	3	2	1	1	4	–	–	–	–	–	–	–	–
General machinery	83	18	11	20	6	10	6	2	2	2	–	3	2	–	1	–	–	–
Electronic and equipment	106	37	22	18	8	6	2	7	4	1	–	–	–	–	–	–	1	–
Electronic components	77	30	8	17	4	1	5	2	9	–	–	1	–	–	–	–	–	1
Transport equipment	18	4	2	–	5	3	1	1	–	–	1	–	–	–	–	–	–	1
Transport equipment parts	51	19	6	3	8	3	3	2	–	1	3	2	1	–	–	–	–	–
Precision instruments	39	12	6	10	1	–	3	1	1	1	–	1	1	1	–	1	–	–
Other	48	19	4	3	2	3	2	2	1	5	2	1	1	1	1	1	–	–
Design centres and R&D bases	264 (65)	83 (19)	34 (8)	53 (18)	26 (2)	14 (4)	16 (4)	16 (4)	7 (1)	3	–	5 (1)	4 (3)	–	1 (1)	–	–	1

The numbers of design centres and R&D bases have been counted separately and are indicated in the separate item above.

Figures in brackets indicate numbers of independent facilities

Source: JETRO 1994

17

Exhibit 2.7: Inward investment – numbers of projects, 1993-94						
	In France		In UK		In Netherlands	
Source	No.	%	No.	%	No.	%
Europe	159	58.9	159	39.4	38	54.3
Asia	21	7.8	30 (from Japan)	7.4	21	30
North America	89	33	196	48.5	10	14.3
Other	1	0.3	19	4.7	1	1.4
Total	270	100	404	100	70	100
Source: Development agencies' annual reports						

Compared to other regions of the world, Europe experiences a higher level of greenfield investment from the US

The origins of inward investment into Europe

The largest foreign investment decision for many years in Europe was witnessed in 1994, with Samsung's announcement of a new consumer electronics plant in the UK which may eventually create up to 3,000 jobs. This was, however, just one of a number of significant inward investment projects in Europe in 1994 (see Exhibit 2.3).

While investments from the Far East – and to a lesser degree the US – make the headlines, intra-European investments represent a far greater source of FDI in the European Union. Around 50 per cent of intra-European FDI originates from Germany, France and the UK. Although its importance differs from country to country, it often represents a more fruitful source of investment projects than some Far East investments. However, much intra-European investment tends to be acquisition or on-going investment in existing plants rather than greenfield projects.

In terms of greenfield investment projects, there are relatively few in any one year. During 1993, for instance, Ernst & Young's annual survey of US outward investment projects identified just 71 new greenfield manufacturing investments worldwide by public limited companies, while the Japanese External Trade Organisation (JETRO) identified 30 Japanese investments in the whole of Europe.

The destination of inward investment into Europe

France, the UK and Belgium/Luxembourg are the main recipients of FDI in Europe. A second tier of major beneficiaries is made up of Spain,

Exhibit 2.8: Percentage share of total manufacturing employment taken by foreign affiliates				
	Total	Chemicals	Computers	Automobile
	%	%	%	%
France	23.8	37.3	54.9	24.4
Finland	4.8	9.3	n/a	1.3
Germany	7.2	11.3	55.9	16.6
Ireland	44.2	70.3	92.9	18.1
Turkey	3.2	7.7	n/a	48.9
UK	16.2	33.4	54.0	40.8
Source: OECD *The Performance of Foreign Affiliates in OECD Countries*, 1994				

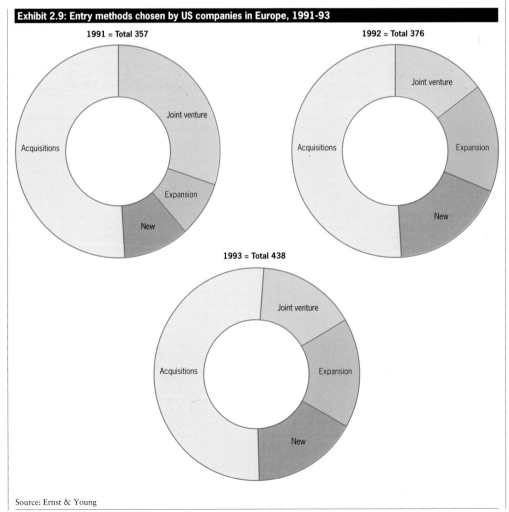

Exhibit 2.9: Entry methods chosen by US companies in Europe, 1991-93

1991 = Total 357

Joint venture · Expansion · New · Acquisitions

1992 = Total 376

Joint venture · Expansion · New · Acquisitions

1993 = Total 438

Joint venture · Expansion · New · Acquisitions

Source: Ernst & Young

The opening up of the former communist countries has increased competition for greenfield and joint-venture projects

Germany and the Netherlands. Ireland, though not included in the data, is also a significant beneficiary. In Eastern Europe, only Hungary and the former Czechoslovakia have managed to attract investment on any scale.

The opening up of the former communist countries of Europe – in particular the Czech Republic, Poland and Hungary – has increased competition for new greenfield and joint-venture projects (JVs). In 1992, approximately 20 per cent of US investments in Europe went to former communist bloc countries.

The Japanese appear more cautious about investing in Eastern Europe, however. The UK, France and Germany receive the lion's share of

Exhibit 2.10: Investment by mode, 1993-94

	France		UK		Netherlands	
	No.	%	No.	%	No.	%
Greenfield	162	60.0	119	29.4	67	95.7
Expansion	68	25.2	207	51.3	3	4.3
Acquisitions	40	14.8	68	16.8	-	-
Joint Venture	-	-	10	2.5	-	-
Total	270	100	404	100	70	100

Source: Development agencies' annual reports

Japanese investment in Europe (see Exhibit 2.6). Second-tier locations again include Spain, the Netherlands, Italy, Belgium and Ireland.

Focusing on a number of the main countries attracting inward investment (for whom data is published), the UK seems an impressive performer (Exhibit 2.7). France and the UK received the same number of projects from within Europe, but a far greater number of US firms invested in the UK. The UK also received the majority of investment from the Far East: most of the projects classified as 'other' in Exhibit 2.7 are from this region.

The importance of FDI varies according to country and sector, with countries such as Ireland heavily dependent for manufacturing employment on foreign companies (see Exhibit 2.8).

Greenfield, joint venture or acquisition?

The available information on the mode of FDI into Europe is contradictory, but this can largely be explained by the objectives of the organisations collecting such data. Ernst & Young's survey (US Manufacturing Abroad 1993) shows that for US investments in Europe, the most popular route is via acquisition, which accounted for 51 per cent of all projects in 1991, 1992 and 1993 (see Exhibit 2.9). Investment via joint ventures, greenfield projects and expansion of existing facilities was at approximately the same level in 1992 and 1993, accounting for 15-17 per cent.

Compared to other regions of the world, Europe experiences a higher level of greenfield and expansion investment from the United States, while US investment into Asia is typified by joint ventures, and in Canada and Mexico by acquisitions.

Data provided by major European development agencies gives a different view. A review of annual reports indicates that greenfield investments account for a far greater proportion of investment in France and the Netherlands than shown in our US survey. This is largely accounted for by the fact that acquisitions and JVs are not the traditional target of such agencies.

Whilst Exhibit 2.7 indicates that the UK attracts the greatest number of projects, Exhibit 2.10 clearly shows that this record is attributable to the very high number of expansion projects. These are 'captured' by the Invest in Britain Bureau's aftercare programme, which is directed

The UK has been the most successful European country in attracting Japanese investment

Exhibit 2.11: US investment in Europe by sector, 1993 – number of projects

Food and beverages 54
Industrial machinery 54
Chemicals 81
Electronics 50
Instruments 45
Other 115
Transportation 33

Source: Ernst & Young

The Japanese appear more cautious about investing in Eastern Europe

19

Exhibit 2.12: Number of overseas electronics production facilities of Japanese corporations, 1992

	Consumer electronic equipment	Industrial electronic equipment	Electronic components and devices
UK	14	18	23
Germany	11	7	20
France	11	10	4
Spain	5	1	3
Ireland	–	2	5
Belgium	1	–	2
Italy	3	2	1
Netherlands	–	2	2
Others	1	–	2
Europe	46	42	62
US	34	45	8
Canada	3	–	5
Puerto Rico	1	–	2
North America	38	45	85
Malaysia	37	13	83
Taiwan	21	12	67
Singapore	20	9	47
Thailand	21	11	36
Republic of Korea	7	9	52
China	8	13	26
Hong Kong	3	4	16
Philippines	5	3	9
Indonesia	8	1	6
India	4	1	1
Others	1	–	3
Asia	135	76	348
Brazil	7	6	13
Mexico	7	3	15
Others	10	1	2
Latin America	24	10	30
Oceania	3	3	1
Africa	4	1	–

Source: Electronics Industries Association of Japan

at securing 'mobile' expansion projects and safeguarding employment during rationalisations.

Additional information from Denmark and Spain indicates that only 6 per cent and 9 per cent respectively of FDI in these countries is greenfield investment. Approximately 40 per cent is related to mergers and acquisitions, with the remainder being additional investment in existing companies.

Sector of investment

Ernst & Young's analysis of outward US investment identifies six main sectors accounting for 74 per cent of all projects. These are, in order of size, chemicals, food, industrial machinery, electronics, instrumentation and transportation equipment (Exhibit 2.11). Within the chemical and food sectors, greenfield operations are common. The electronic/computer sector is typified by acquisitions and joint ventures, while the industrial and transportation sectors have a more even establishment mode.

Japanese investments tend to be in similar sectors, with the exception of food. JETRO's statistics (Exhibit 2.6) illustrate not only key differences between countries' successes by industrial sector, but also the propensity of certain countries to attract particular sectors. The UK has been the most successful European country in attracting Japanese investment, but it has been notably unsuccessful in attracting pharmaceutical and food projects. France has been most successful in the food sector, Italy in textiles, Germany in precision engineering, Ireland in electronics and the Benelux countries in chemicals.

Prospects for FDI in the late 1990s

The prospects for inward investment from key countries/regions forms a vital element in the marketing strategies of inward investment agencies. Notable developments in these main source regions/countries which will affect the immediate future of FDI are outlined below.

Countries of origin

United States
● The number of investments are increasing as the economic upturn progresses, but they are generally of a smaller scale than previously. The '1992 effect' is wearing off and investment flows into Western Europe are not likely to return to their former high levels;
● US companies' attention will also focus on other regions, including Mexico (because of the North American Free Trade Agreement, NAFTA), Eastern Europe (which is receiving around 20 per cent of US investment in Europe), the Pacific Rim and South East Asia, where economic growth has been double that of Europe and Latin America;
● Sectors experiencing significant development include biotechnology, aerospace, composites, electronic systems, software, integrated circuits, electronic materials and artificial intelligence.

Japan
● Large-scale Japanese investment in the late 1980s was ahead of what might have been expected due to concerns over 'Fortress Europe';
● The strong yen and the decline of export competitiveness will increase pressure to invest directly in Europe, though the timing of such investment will depend on the domestic economic situation;
● Japanese investment is likely to spread throughout Europe rather than concentrating in the UK, as Japanese companies look for market access and seek to satisfy a desire to be seen as more European;
● Japanese companies are also looking at South East Asian locations such as China, Thailand and Vietnam, which are rapidly opening up to foreign investment;
● Sectors experiencing significant development include structural ceramics, consumer electronics, automotive components, low-cost manufacturing, semi-conductor equipment technologies, electronic peripherals/components and image recognition;
● As Exhibit 2.12 illustrates, Japanese investment in electronics is predominantly located in Asia;
● Japanese firms are among the most heavily targeted by inward investment promoters.

Other Asian economies
● Much has been written about the prospects for FDI from the newly industrialising countries (NICs) of South East Asia. Given their economic growth it would seem reasonable to expect outward investment from this region;
● Investment from the NICs is occurring, but it is

limited in origin and is selective in destination and sector. Competition – both from within the region itself and from developed nations – is intensive. Moreover, the attraction of FDI is still a significant focus of economic policy within these countries;

● For Korean and Taiwanese companies, there are still important market opportunities within their own region, and investments abroad have tended to be constrained by trade restrictions. Additionally, few companies possess the ability to internationalise, and experience to date has largely been via marketing subsidiaries;

● Singapore and Hong Kong, which share similar characteristics, have both undertaken a remarkable level of investment in China.

Taiwan

● Taiwan is currently one of the most fruitful sources of FDI from the Asian NICs, and is likely to remain so;

● It has experienced high growth rates, has a strong current account surplus, and is increasing its level of exports to Europe;

● Companies in Taiwan are increasingly constrained by the price and availability of land, and to a lesser degree labour, in sectors such as electrical, electronic and chemical engineering and mechanical design.

South Korea

● South Korea now has a more favourable government attitude to outward investment. Moreover, internal pressures due to high labour costs will force companies to internationalise;

● Exports to the EU have grown, and South Korea has a high current account surplus and high savings ratio;

● The economy is dominated by large conglomerates ('chaebols') and the number of potential investors is therefore small, making the targeting of decision-makers particularly important.

Western Europe

● The UK economy is in its third year of growth after a deep recession and historically it has been a major source of FDI. However, much of this investment is via acquisition;

● The German economy continues to suffer from the impact and cost of reunification. Companies are under significant cost pressure to relocate or to undertake new manufacturing operations elsewhere. Eastern Europe is high on the list of potential locations for investment;

● European-based companies undertaking significant development include those in telecoms, automotive, plastics, chemicals and software;

● The votes by Norway and Switzerland not to join the EU and the EEA respectively have led to a growing number of companies in those countries considering locating operations within the EU.

Destination countries

The former communist countries of Europe

● Given the size, location and scale of change, developments in the former communist bloc represent a significant potential influence on FDI;

● The majority of foreign investment to date has been to participate in the privatisation process and to access new markets via acquisition and joint ventures;

● Many of the states have skilled and educated workforces; labour is relatively low cost; access to Western European markets (especially Germany) is good; and in many cases there are strong historical links with Western countries;

● Some companies have already recognised that the region may be an attractive location in which to be based. This will be increasingly the case if the countries are granted membership of, or greater access to, the markets of Western Europe;

● In the short term, however, there aspects of some of these countries which may deter inward investors. These include political instability, 'cultural dissonance' between the workforce and foreign companies, and an insufficiently developed banking and credit system;

● These factors are recognised by the emerging inward investment agencies in the various states and, provided the processes of reform continue, are unlikely to be long-term obstacles to FDI. A number of countries in Eastern/Central Europe therefore represent a threat to Western Europe in the attraction of investment in the late 1990s.

North Africa and the Middle East

● Many Magreb countries such as Tunisia are already actively promoting themselves as low-cost manufacturing bases from which companies can serve the European market. As these countries have labour rates well below those in Europe and offer a large and increasingly well-educated workforce, they are beginning to compete with traditional European locations;

● Increasingly, companies are also considering Israel as a potential location from which to serve Europe. The fast-growing Turkish economy, meanwhile, offers a possible location from which to serve both Eastern Europe and the Asian republics of the former Soviet Union.

European integration

The perceived requirement for foreign companies to be within the EU by 1 January 1993 may have lent a certain urgency to companies' strategies from the late 1980s and caused some projects to be brought forward. As a result we may now witness a slight slowing of FDI projects into the EU.

The entry of three European Free Trade Association (EFTA) countries into the EU may represent a threat to the prospects of FDI into existing EU member states. A recent Ernst & Young survey found that Japanese companies in particular were far more likely to invest in the EFTA countries if they joined the EU.

The present economic situation and the continued integration and expansion of the EU has prompted multinational companies to concentrate on improving the efficiency of their existing operations rather than investing in new locations.

The year 2000 and beyond

Inward investment promotion agencies should now be looking beyond the year 2000 to understand the world in which they will soon be operating. They will need to focus on the market opportunities available to companies and the means (including location) by which they can exploit them. The underlying issues shaping corporate locations include:

● Global forces: institutional and economic forces such as rate of economic growth, development of trading blocs, emergence and pace of deregulation and privatisation, and capital flows;

Countries such as Tunisia are actively promoting themselves as low-cost bases from which companies can serve the European market

● Home and host country positions;
● Technology, particularly information technology
● Corporate strategies, management, organisation.

Global forces which determine the overall operating environment (providing opportunities and constraints) will shape the form, size, depth and spread of technological and corporate developments. Technological development will enable and often drive changes in corporate strategy, management and organisation. This in turn will have implications for the location of facilities.

Corporations will develop by:
● Increasingly adopting flat, flexible structures;
● Benefiting from a multi-cultural approach;
● Developing strategic partnerships such as JVs and alliances to reduce the risks and time involved in market entry;
● Developing outsourcing of production and service delivery;
● Adopting a flexible approach to the scope of production/services;
● Requiring local managers to be entrepreneurial so that they in turn will require more decision-making responsibility;
● Being more responsive to industrial customer requirements and reducing cycle times.

Such an approach can only be facilitated by improved information technology. In general terms this involves the costs, power, means and speed of information transfer becoming, respectively, cheaper, larger, smaller and faster, at a greater pace than ever before. As a result, corporations will be able to manage and integrate operations that are increasingly geographically and functionally diverse. This could mean that 'location' will have an enhanced or reduced importance in the exploitation of opportunities. For example:
● Integration of operations may reduce the need for duplication of functions in numerous locations;
● Demand for customisation may place more emphasis on market proximity in order to reduce cycle times;
● Access to human production resources and 'brain power' will increasingly reduce dependence on Europe and North America.

The environment for Western European development agencies will be challenging, as companies develop regionally independent or globally interdependent strategies. Facilities for domestic goods and services may increasingly move abroad and be followed by R&D/management for both foreign and domestic markets. In the longer term, significant destinations (and therefore competitors) could include South Africa, India and Latin America (especially Brazil and Argentina). Even if cheap labour and attractive opportunities do not lead companies to new locations, European agencies will have to contend with the changing organisation of production and an increasingly competitive environment.

The future for inward investment agencies
The future for FDI in Europe has significant implications for the inward investment agencies. The most prominent issues they now face include:
● The relatively small number of truly mobile investment projects into and between European countries;

● The growing significance of pan-European production/organisation strategies involving the possibility of large-scale rationalisation programmes and the transfer of production between European plants;
● A growing number of alternative international locations, due to the increased liberalisation of governing regimes;
● The importance of JV and acquisition/merger activity as a mode of foreign investment. This may have negative regional/local effects, as the structure and ownership of enterprises will not provide an appropriate range of options;
● The large numbers of areas and agencies – approximately 1,000 in Europe – which have a remit to attract inward investment;
● The lack, as yet, of a significant number of large-scale investments from the South East Asian NICs, which is especially relevant given the rise in intra-regional FDI in this area;
● The push for more high-tech and skilled operations from countries such as Taiwan, Singapore and Malaysia may attract projects that Western European agencies have traditionally felt were destined for their areas;
● The technology and skills of inward investment promoters have been widely transferred.

Consequently, inward investment agencies are working in an increasingly competitive, difficult and complex world. They must assess:
● The emphasis they place on assisting the existing stock of inward investors and the issues surrounding who should be undertaking such work, which companies to target, the manner in which they are approached and the range of relevant services the agencies can offer them;
● The role they can play in joint ventures and acquisitions, given that these tend to be company-specific rather than location-specific and are traditionally conducted through private sector advisers;
● The range of services that can be provided in a professional manner;
● The means by which they can maximise their effective resources and deliver the required services through co-operation with other public and the private sector organisations;
● The degree to which they develop the skills and knowledge of agency personnel, the type of personnel they recruit, and whether or not they should make a serious attempt to stem the high staff turnover rates that have become characteristic of inward investment agencies;
● The significance attached to the in-house use and development of databases, desktop publishing and project-tracking systems to improve the efficiency of their efforts and as management tools;
● How to cope with the fragmentation of inward investment activities (which causes confusion and irritation because companies do not know whom to deal with) whilst also being seen to 'deliver' for the varied geographical and community interests covered by 'regionally based agencies';
● The best approach and methods to gain maximum benefit from the lobbying of central government in order to serve regional interests;
● Their attitude to co-operation and partnership with development agencies within their own and foreign countries for, as with other businesses, the distinction between competitor and partner is becoming blurred.

> Inward investment agencies are working in an increasingly competitive, difficult and complex world

> Technological development will enable, and often drive, changes in corporate strategy

Chapter 3

HOW COMPANIES MAKE LOCATION DECISIONS

Cross-border location decision-making is a complex process, involving many issues and often stretching over a period of several years. As with other kinds of strategic decision-making, it is also heavily influenced by the personalities involved.

Location decisions are similar to other assessments of large-scale investments, but with the added complication of geographic variability. Because many firms undertake them infrequently, location decisions are often clouded by mystique, confusion and ignorance. They are further complicated by personal prejudices and intense lobbying on the part of development agencies.

This chapter addresses the issues that are important to agencies seeking to attract mobile investment: the reasons why companies invest in new locations, the different types of investment decision, and the various roles of those involved in the decision-making process. It also considers those aspects of the processes that are of interest to companies undertaking such decisions. These are:

● The stages of the location decision process;
● Evaluating location options and information issues;
● Key location factors and their relative importance.

Most of the points made relate to both cross-border and domestic location decisions.

Why companies invest in new locations

A location decision arises out of long-term capacity planning and forms a core element in the fulfilment of a firm's strategic goals. Different locations have the potential to impact significantly on a company's performance, thus affecting revenue, costs, service levels and, most importantly, profitability.

A variety of factors may affect space and location requirements (see Exhibit 3.1). It may be possible to respond to space/location pressures by, for example, making changes in productivity, introducing shift patterns, sub-contracting or refurbishing existing facilities. When these pressures become too great, however, investment/disinvestment location decisions are required.

One of the most significant reasons for such decisions is a change in the market – in its scale, geography, nature or diversity – as well as quality and price issues and competitor activity. Changes in these areas will result in decisions that reflect a company's desire to sustain, protect or create new markets.

> **Different locations have the potential to impact significantly on a firm's strategic goals**

> **Location decisions are often clouded by mystique, confusion and ignorance**

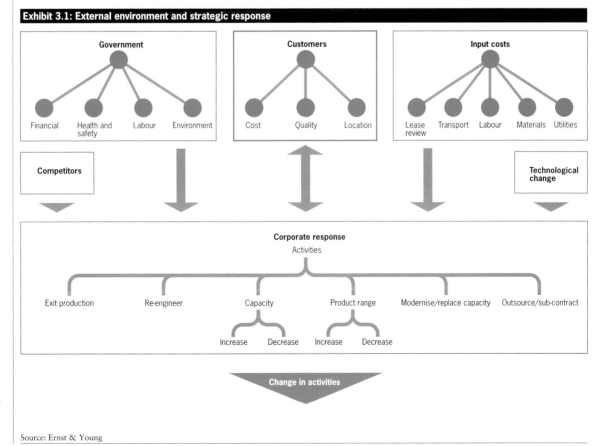

Exhibit 3.1: External environment and strategic response

Source: Ernst & Young

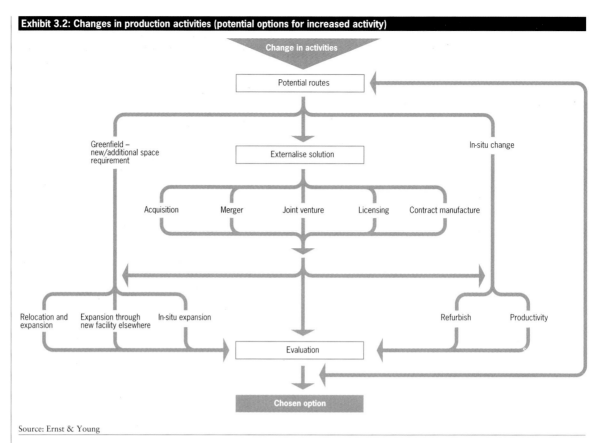

Exhibit 3.2: Changes in production activities (potential options for increased activity)

Source: Ernst & Young

Location
decisions
attract a
great deal
of interest,
sometimes
unwarranted
and
unwanted

In addition to market factors, other significant reasons for foreign investment decisions include a company's desire to find new resources (physical, labour or technological), to make efficiency gains (through cross-border product and process specialisation), or to acquire strategic assets in order to improve international competitiveness. These may be either proactive or defensive decisions and may, of course, be combined. Moreover, they may change over time as the company becomes established in its new location.

Changes in the nature of space/accommodation needs – caused by the introduction of new technology, for example, or by alterations to regulatory, health, safety or environmental requirements – may also trigger location decisions.

The choices involved

The decision to establish additional capacity in a particular area will not necessarily result in new greenfield facilities, even if the company concerned does not have an existing presence in the chosen location.

Frequently, companies will investigate a range of investment modes, including joint ventures, acquisitions and licensing agreements (see Exhibit 3.2), proceeding to a greenfield solution only if these alternative routes prove unworkable. These alternative modes may or may not in turn lead to new capacity or a location decision. The majority of such evaluations tend not to result in the development of a greenfield site in a new location.

When location decisions do arise, for both domestic and foreign firms there is invariably a choice between existing and new sites. Some of the options that need to be taken into account include:
● Changing the scale of production (increasing or decreasing) across a range of locations;

● Increasing production through the creation of additional facilities at a new location or cease production through the closure of one plant;
● Introducing changes in production through relocation, including the transfer of existing production capacity.

Key players in the location decision process

Location decision-making can involve a significant number of personnel or very few. This will depend on, among other things, the culture and size of the organisation concerned. It may also depend on a need for secrecy: a location decision attracts a great deal of interest – both from within the company and from competitors – which is sometimes unwarranted and unwanted, and it can be viewed with suspicion by staff because of the perceived threat to the status quo.

The way in which companies make location decisions, the personnel involved and the roles and responsibilities they assume is of interest to organisations involved in attracting mobile investment because:
● By targeting executives who are involved in making location decisions and by understanding the requirements of 'organisational selling' they are able to influence the selection of areas for consideration and the final location decision;
● By understanding how companies make location decisions (and the factors influencing those decisions), they can provide detailed information where it is needed and therefore pitch their message at the appropriate level.

Not surprisingly, given their importance to company success, location decisions are made at a senior level. The key decision-making role is usually taken by the chairperson/president together with the chief executive/managing director. Divisional heads and finance directors

The decision to establish additional capacity in a particular area will not necessarily result in new greenfield facilities

invariably also form part of the location team. Where they exist, legal and property functions typically provide technical advice but are not necessarily permanent members of the 'team'.

The responsibilities of the key participants are determined by their position in the company and their role in the location search. Exhibit 3.3 illustrates these varying positions and roles.

Exhibit 3.3: Key positions and roles in location decisions

Chairperson/ president/CEO	Suggest countries, define criteria, evaluate options
Division head/finance	Collect data, give technical advice, evaluate options
Legal/property	Collect data, give technical advice

Stages in the location decision process

Location decisions involve a number of stages which may be revisited as personalities and the operating environment changes. (They are set out in a simplified form in Exhibit 3.4.) The stages of the location decision process include:

● The 'conception stage' – it is recognised that there is a need to change production capacity and so a proposal is formed to evaluate an investment;
● The 'defining stage' – the option of investing in a foreign country is evaluated, project and goals are defined and basic criteria established;
● The 'decision stage' – locations are evaluated and a decision is made;
● Development negotiations – agreement is reached on utility, labour, incentives, taxation, etc.
● Implementation – commencement of operations.

Exhibit 3.4: The location decision process

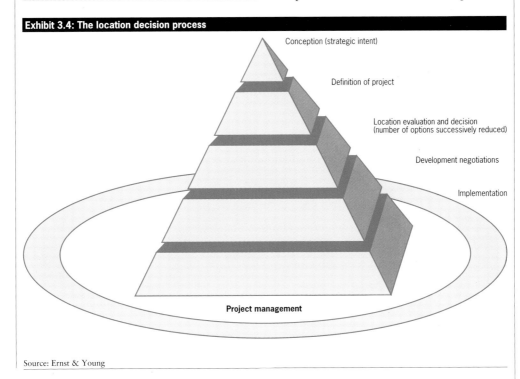

Source: Ernst & Young

Exhibit 3.5: Key location success factors

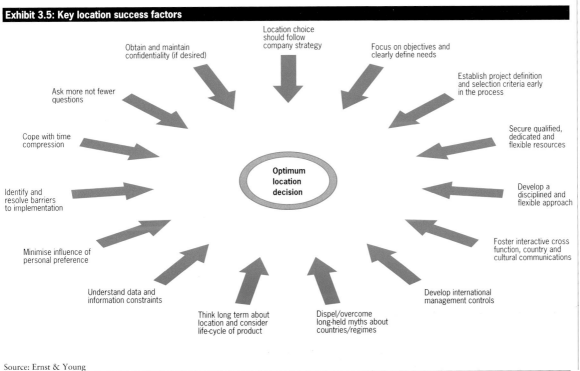

Source: Ernst & Young

Recognition of the need to make a location decision can occur at many levels in the corporate hierarchy

The conception and defining phases

The conception and defining stages involve the recognition of a need to review production strategy, the establishment of operational, organisational, financial and human resource goals, and the subsequent definition of project parameters and basic evaluation criteria.

The stimulus for these stages may be external or internal, or it may be the result of ad hoc planning (a plant manager reacting to problems of capacity, for example) or a formal planning system identifying future production over- or under-capacity.

The type of decision needed will differ according to the source of stimulus. Ad hoc/'bottom-up' needs are likely to involve changes in production capacity, while corporate/'top-down' planning will typically involve 'strategic' issues such as the approval of new plants or acquisitions. These distinctions are, of course, over-simplifications: recognition of the need to make a location decision can occur at many different levels in the corporate hierarchy simultaneously, and all these levels may be consulted in the corporate/'top-down' approach.

It is at this stage that the members of the 'location team' should be selected. Once they have assumed their respective roles, they can help to refine the project parameters and key location considerations.

The correct formulation of these elements is vital to a successful location search. Selection needs to follow strategy, and agreement on criteria must be reached at an early stage. This will also help to minimise the influence of the decision-makers' personal preferences. However, these criteria will inevitably evolve as the team progresses through the sequence of location decisions.

In defining 'the project', companies need to: address corporate objectives and project parameters; agree and define the key location factors to be taken into consideration; understand the availability and limitations of data/information. (All these issues are dealt with in more detail later in this chapter.)

Exhibit 3.6: Project parameters to be established
● Site (physical qualities of facility)
● Labour
● Geographic – accessibility and proximity to materials, markets, modes of transport
● Finance

The decision stage: location evaluation

For many companies, the decision stage will involve a number of steps during which the range of potential locations is progressively reduced until a specific site or premises is selected. Typically:
● Almost 75 per cent of companies select a country first and then choose a region or specific site;
● In approximately 25 per cent of cases, the final location choice is between regions in different countries.

The location decision-making process is, of course, considerably more complex and more variable than this implies, since companies are frequently involved in a number of sub-decisions within the overall decision process (Exhibit 3.7).

Almost 75 per cent of companies select a country first and then choose a region or specific site

Exhibit 3.7: Different approaches to location evaluation	
	%
● Long list of four or more countries narrowed down to a shortlist of two or three countries	25
● Specific country or region(s) within a single country selected from a list of countries	40
● Specific (sub-) region selected within a country	46
● Regions or sub-regions within several countries selected from a list of countries	16
● Specific (sub-) region selected from a list of (sub-) regions in several countries	26
● Specific city/sub-region selected within a region	40

Source: *New Location Factors*, European Commission 1992 (survey conducted by Ernst & Young)

Development agencies need to be aware of the decision sequence outlined above: it will inform them of their likely competitors and the nature of messages they should be using when addressing relocating companies.

The range and the relative importance of various location factors will inevitably change as this sequence of decisions progresses. These factors are discussed in detail under the section 'Key Location Factors'.

Location options and information issues

Companies face significant difficulties in defining the appropriate criteria by which to make location decisions. Some of the most common problems concerned with information-gathering are shown in Exhibit 3.8 (below).

The sources of information and advice available to assist in the evaluation of locations are varied. Typically, different sources will be used at different stages in the location evaluation process, and will in part be determined by whether the need is for exploration/investigation or for confirmation of facts and views. Five main

Exhibit 3.8: Typical information problems
● Lack of consistency over time, between countries and regions
● Geographical information available does not cover precise study areas
● Lack of transparency over meaning
● Lack of real timeliness of data – information is often dated; companies need forecasts as well as current information

Exhibit 3.9: Types of information to be combined	
Quantitative – financial	
Costs	Fixed one-off – site development
	Continuous – operating costs
Incentives	Grants
	Loans
	Training
	Taxation
Quantitative – indicators	
Gateway (that is, the essential attribute a location must possess)	Presence of – yes/no
	If no, location automatically disregarded
Performance quality	Interruption of utility supplies
	Number of strikes
	Extent of collective bargaining
	Speed with which planning permission can be obtained
Availability	Number unemployed
	Number of relevant skilled workers
Qualitative factors	
Attitudinal	Political and government – welcome and ease of doing business

Selection needs to follow strategy, and agreement on criteria must be reached at an early stage

Exhibit 3.10: Evaluation tools

Evaluation tool	Characteristic	Main issue
Payback	Maximum time over which investment expenditure must be recovered. Can be short: 2-3 years	Definition of 'investment outlay' is ambiguous and can therefore be manipulated. Cashflows that arise outside the payback period are ignored. Useful to measure risk but not profit
Rate of return	A certain percentage return which the investment expenditure must generate for the proposal to be accepted	Not indicative of whether the project is wealth-creating; only provides an estimate of the rate of return capital. Also in calculation, companies need to consider: is return pre- or post-tax? How is depreciation accounted for? Are assets to be included at original cost or net of depreciation?
Internal rate of return	A firm calculates the projected rate of return on the capital invested in the project over its life. The aim is to find a percentage rate of discount that will reduce the present value of the sequence of cashflows to the same values as the case invested in the project	Multiple internal rates of return may exist whereby the decision rule breaks down. A project with a higher rate of return may not always be better than a project with a lower rate of return, as the amount originally invested may be different. Also, the rate of return in effect assumes reinvestment at the project's own (internal) rate of return, which may not be the opportunity cost of capital, therefore making it hard to compare two different projects especially if they have different lives
Net present value	A firm chooses a minimum acceptable rate of return and using that rate calculates the present value of the future cashflows. If the present value is less than the amount of the original investment, the project does not meet the minimum rate of return and should be rejected	This assumes the firm can estimate the discounted value of the future services from the investment. Calculations involved are often costly and complicated
Weighted scoring models	These assign weights to location factors. Each alternative is evaluated on each factor, then multiplied by weights which are totalled for each site. Weights can be assigned objectively (based on percentages of total costs where appropriate) or subjectively (judgement decisions are involved)	Subjectivity of assigning weight factors. Large number of different 'types' of data causes difficulty of comparing like with like
Logistics modelling	Supply-chain analysis and linear programming	Focusing on distribution. This is therefore inappropriate for certain activities and needs to be part of a wider location evaluation

Source: Sheenan 1994, Mott 1989

groupings of sources of information are evident. These include:
● Business-related – subsidiaries, customers, suppliers and JV partners;
● Promotion agencies – embassies, governments and development agencies;
● Business relationships – bankers, lawyers, estate agents and accountants;
● Business organisations – employers' associations and chambers of commerce;
● Location advisers – management, production or property-based.

These potential players all have different merits and experience/knowledge to offer. Some will provide their services free, some can be trusted, others should be greeted with scepticism. It is therefore important that companies understand the motives of those from whom they are seeking information. Organisations seeking to attract inward investment will rarely lie, but their use of information may be subjective and omissions are frequent.

Once companies have selected their criteria and identified the limitations of the data available to them, they are then faced with the problem of combining many different types of information to produce a composite and comparative picture.

Evaluation tools
Various approaches can be undertaken to evaluate location options. Most companies undertake a combination of financial and qualitative analysis. The use of different evaluation techniques is often guided by: the size of the investment and company concerned; parent company requirements; whether or not government assistance is sought; the nature of the project in question; the stage in the evaluation process; and the relative merits of the different techniques.

Multinationals, their subsidiaries and large domestic firms have a high propensity to use financial techniques (including discounted cash-flow analysis, internal rate of return, net present value and payback methods). Subsidiaries are also likely to use more than one method of financial analysis, as the parent company may wish to demonstrate a particular case through the use of a chosen evaluation technique.

Financial evaluations are, however, less frequently used when investment decisions are related to replacement or modernisation, when they are small in value, or when the investment does not involve an application for financial assistance. Different types of projects may rely more heavily on certain methods of analysis: the selection of a site for a distribution operation, for example, will rely heavily on computerised logistics models.

The stage of evaluation also affects the appropriateness of the evaluation techniques used. Various weight-scoring models can be used in the early stages of the location decision-making process in order to generate a list of feasible options. These can then be evaluated on a more

It is important to understand the motives of those from whom information is sought

Companies are faced with the problem of combining different types of information to produce a composite and comparative picture

Exhibit 3.11: Key location factors and their relative importance

A: Choice of country: for example, Austria

Key location factors	Significant influences	Wild cards
Proximity to markets.	Transport costs.	Industrial relations.
Labour: ● cost;	Air and road transport.	Economic stability.
● availability;	Government attitude	Environmental legislation.
● quality.	to inward investment.	Restrictions on foreign
Existence of other	Incentives.	labour.
operations.	Premises/site availability.	
Management preferences.	Location of suppliers.	
Fiscal issues and taxation:	Language.	
● corporate tax;	Location of competitors	
● transfer of earnings	and their reaction.	
● restrictions;		
● capital restrictions.		

Incentives and development activity become important in decisions between regions, whether or not they are in the same country

B: Choice of region: Lower Austria

Key location factors	Significant influences	Wild cards
Proximity to markets.	Labour quality.	Availability of specific skills.
Site/premises availability.	Air transport.	Industrial relations.
Labour availability.	Government attitude	
Incentives.	to inward investment.	
Road transport.	Site/premises costs.	
	Transport costs.	
	Location of suppliers.	
	Location of competitors.	

C: Choice of site: St Pölten, Lower Austria

Site selection factors

Site characteristics:
● Levelness;
● Other users;
● Services available;
● Expansion potential.

Environmental impact/planning restrictions:
● Availability of amenities;
● Management preferences.

The legacy of the past creates the need for more in-depth analysis of many of the former communist countries

selective financial basis. Some of the major evaluation tools and their principal characteristics are illustrated in Exhibit 3.10 (above).

Key location factors

This section discusses the key location factors that companies consider when making location decisions.

Location factors vary enormously between companies and the key to understanding them is an appreciation of each particular firm's objectives and needs. The range of factors taken into account and their importance will also depend on the stage reached in the decision-making process. Some of the key determinants explaining the relative importance of location factors are shown in Exhibit 3.12 (below).

Exhibit 3.12: Factors determining importance of location criteria

● Strategic reasons for the location decision
● Size of the investing company and operation to be undertaken
● Culture of company and individuals making the decision
● Countries under investigation
● Function of operation and inter-company relationships, i.e. distribution/manufacturing, independent/interdependent
● Time-sensitivity of decision

Focusing on manufacturing operations, three groups of influences on location decisions have been identified and are illustrated in Exhibit 3.11. These include:
● *Key location factors*. Factors shown to be of relative importance with a high degree of consistency;
● *Significant influences*. Factors which are less

important but which again emerge consistently in a number of studies;
● *Wild cards*. Factors which have a significant influence on decisions in a small number of location studies.

It is clear that broadly similar factors are taken into account in both country and regional decisions, though their relative importance varies and specific site characteristics come into play in the final choice of land or property. In addition:
● Incentives and development activity become important in decisions between regions, whether or not these are in the same country;
● The availability and cost of premises play a significant role in decisions about where to site a new operation within a region or country.

Former communist countries

Many former communist countries in Central and Eastern Europe continue to make progress towards a market-oriented economy and enjoy economic and political stability. However, the legacy of their past creates the need for more in-depth analysis and greater consideration of certain location issues. Some of these are set out in Exhibit 3.13, below.

Exhibit 3.13: Location in Eastern Europe

● Prospects for entry into European Union
● Import and export regulations – tariffs and quotas
● Regional trading regimes
● Intellectual property – framework and enforcement
● Due diligence and timescale in property acquisition
● Form of property ownership
● Availability of appropriate property and sites
● Infrastructure facilities
● Access to raw materials, components and utilities
● Attitude of community to foreign investments
● Understanding of local culture and attitudes
● Maturity of financial markets
● Availability and quality of workforce including management
● Mobility of workforce
● Some information/statistical needs

POLITICAL AND ECONOMIC OVERVIEW

Political uncertainties continue to have a very significant impact on the climate in which businesses operate in several countries

The successful creation of the European Economic Area (EEA) on 1 January 1993 resulted in the world's largest trading bloc, comprising a population of more than 360 million and accounting for some 60 per cent of world trade among its 18 member states. The formation of the EEA means that the regulations and directives of the European Union (EU) are applied across a wider geographical area than ever before, and that the European economy is increasingly integrated and inter-dependent.

Sweden, Finland and Austria agreed in referenda in 1994 to join the EU, and their influence is already reflected in the composition of the European Commission, which has now been expanded to accommodate the new member countries. Norway, however, voted against EU membership, while Switzerland voted against membership of the EEA.

In addition to these developments, a number of countries outside the EEA have completed association agreements (or other less formal agreements on trade and co-operation) with the European Union, making the consistency of political and legal approaches more extensive (see Exhibit 4.1, below).

Exhibit 4.1: European political structures

European Union (EU) members	EEA members	Association agreements/ potential EU members
Austria	EU members plus:	Bulgaria
Belgium	Iceland	Cyprus
Denmark	Liechtenstein	Czech Republic
Finland	Norway	Hungary
France		Malta
Germany		Poland
Greece		Romania
Ireland		Slovakia
Italy		Turkey
Luxembourg		
The Netherlands		
Portugal		
Spain		
Sweden		
UK		

Although these structures and organisations provide a basis of social and economic stability among member countries, political uncertainties continue to have a very significant impact on the climate in which businesses operate in several European countries. This is true in economically developed nations as well as in the emerging economies. The fall of the government in Italy, amid continuing political and administrative reforms there, has created a climate of continuing uncertainty. Domestic political factors have also created considerable uncertainty recently in Spain, Ireland and the UK. While the instability created by the various referenda on EU membership has passed, a degree of adjustment will be required during the transition of the countries concerned to full EU membership. This will affect both new members and old.

The benefits of closer economic and political links between Eastern European countries and the West are beginning to be seen in the emerging economies. Many Central and Eastern European countries have experienced strong growth in exports, mainly to Western Europe. Exports from Poland and Slovakia, for example, have increased by approximately 20 per cent. Exports of manufactured goods from the Czech Republic have also increased.

Set against these positive trends, however, is the continuing risk that the need to ensure competitiveness may have a negative impact on traditional industries and employment in many Eastern European countries. This appears to be the case in Russia (though indicators here are contradictory and less reliable than in some other states), where output has declined, particularly in defence-related industries, contributing to growing social, political and economic uncertainty.

Economic interdependence increases

The abolition of physical and technical barriers to trade across wide areas of Europe is increasingly creating a network of economic, financial and political interdependence. Growing trade and increased levels of foreign direct investment into Central and Eastern Europe are likely to spread the benefits of political co-operation and economic convergence.

The prospects for a Europe-wide economic recovery are closely tied to German economic performance. The Ernst & Young ITEM Club has forecast that stronger growth in Germany in 1995 will assist recovery in several other European states, notably the Netherlands and Belgium, which are likely to benefit from direct trade with Germany.

In other European countries such as Italy, Spain and France, growth is likely to be concurrent with Germany's. The goal of Economic and Monetary Union (EMU), reiterated by the Maastricht Treaty, emphasises this growing convergence. The EMU timetable provides for the launch of a single European currency and the creation of a European Central Bank by January 1999 at the latest, provided economic convergence between member states continues. In fact, the core European economies of Austria, Germany, France, the Netherlands and Luxembourg are expected to meet the Maastricht criteria by 1997, which would therefore present the opportunity for an early move towards the third stage of monetary union – that is, a single

Increased levels of foreign direct investment into Eastern Europe are likely to spread the benefits of economic convergence

Exhibit 4.2: Contenders for the single currency

	Gross debt % of GDP			Budget deficit % of GDP			Inflation %			Long-term interest rates %			Overall Pass/Fail
	94	95	Pass/Fail	94	95	Pass/Fail	94	95	Pass/Fail	94	95	Pass/Fail	Pass/Fail
Inner core													
Germany	51	59	√	5.6	3.6	x	3.0	2.3	√	6.9	6.9	√	x
Netherlands	81	82	x	3.8	3.6	x	1.9	1.9	√	7.0	6.9	√	x
Austria	58	60	√	4.2	5.0	x	3.1	2.6	√	6.8	7.0	√	x
Luxembourg	9	10	√	1.3	1.6	√	2.3	3.0	√	–	–	–	√
Outer core													
France	50	52	√	5.5	4.7	x	1.7	1.8	√	7.5	6.8	√	x
Belgium	146	145	x	5.8	4.7	x	2.4	2.5	√	7.8	7.2	√	x
Denmark	82	83	x	4.2	3.0	√	1.8	2.4	√	7.9	7.7	√	x
Special cases													
Ireland	92	87	x	2.3	2.0	√	2.5	2.5	√	8.1	7.5	√	x
UK	53	55	√	4.8	2.5	√	2.4	2.9	√	8.2	7.4	√	√
Periphery													
Italy	122	125	x	10.6	9.4	x	3.9	3.6	x	10.6	10.9	x	x
Finland	80	80	x	4.6	5.1	x	1.7	2.1	√	9.0	8.6	√	x
Sweden	94	103	x	11.2	10.2	x	2.0	2.4	√	8.4	10.0	x	x
Portugal	81	82	x	7.1	6.6	x	4.6	4.3	x	10.8	10.5	x	x
Spain	64	68	x	7.0	6.5	x	4.6	4.4	x	9.8	10.5	x	x
Greece	118	119	x	13.1	11.6	x	11.1	9.9	x	18.9	19.5	x	x

Pass/fail is based on 1995 estimates

Maastricht economic convergence criteria

Countries must comply with the following:

● Fiscal discipline – governments' financial positions must be sustainable; the annual budget deficit must be no more than 3 per cent of gross domestic product (GDP); outstanding government debt must be no more than 60 per cent of GDP

● Price stability – annual inflation rate must not be more than 1.5 per cent above the average rate in the three countries with the lowest rate of inflation

● Interest rates – to indicate the durability of a member state's convergence, long-term interest rates must be no more than 2 per cent above the average rate on 10-year government bonds in the three countries with the lowest inflation rates

● Exchange rate – must have been stable within the Exchange Rate Mechanism during the preceding two years (i.e. no devaluation).

Source: *The European*, 1995

European currency. In many countries, however (as Exhibit 4.2 illustrates), inflation rates and government deficits are currently incompatible with EMU requirements. Moreover, a number of countries remain sceptical about the whole idea.

Growth in Europe

Economic recovery in most Western Europe countries is now firmly established, following a prolonged period of tentative growth. While the overall growth rate is projected by the OECD to be around 3 per cent in 1995 and 1996, there are likely to be significant regional variations.

In Central Europe, most countries are now experiencing positive growth. Hungary, Poland and Slovakia, for example, have had recent short-term growth rates of up to 5 per cent, while Bulgaria and Romania have had more modest growth of 1-2 per cent year on year. Output is projected to rise gradually in most of these countries year on year in the medium term. It should be borne in mind, however, that this significant rise has come about after a number of years of massive decreases in economic activity.

A number of European countries – notably Ireland, the UK, Denmark, Finland and Norway – have been experiencing solid growth in economic output for some time now. Continental European countries, which went into recession later, are experiencing growth at a later stage. It is projected that in the future, some of the fastest growing continental economies will be found in southern Europe, notably Portugal and Spain. This reflects not only the potential of these countries for further economic development, but also the boost they will receive from

Exhibit 4.3: Economic output – Central and Eastern Europe

	Percentage change over previous year			
	1993	1994	1995	1996
Bulgaria	–4.2	+1.0	+2.0	+2.0
Czech Republic	–0.3	+3.0	+4.0	+5.0
Hungary	–2.3	+2.5	+0.5	+1.0
Poland	+3.8	+4.0	+5.0	+5.0
Romania	–1.3	+1.0	+1.5	+2.0
Russia	–12.0	–15.0	–7.0	+0.0
Slovakia	–4.1	+3.5	+4.0	+5.0

Source: *OECD Economic Outlook* 1994

continuing high levels of investment from European Commission programmes.

In most Western and Eastern European economies, exports have been the primary engine of growth. Ireland, Portugal, Spain, the UK, Finland, Germany, Belgium and the Netherlands, for example, have all experienced a strong surge in demand for exports.

Consumer-led recovery has, however, been more tentative. An exception to this pattern is France, where the personal sector seems to be leading the domestic revival due to an increase in disposable income sufficient to support spending (following a prolonged period of cuts in consumer spending over the past five years). France's situation contrasts with the experience in Germany, where consumer spending is projected to lag behind economic recovery. A significant factor affecting the situation in Germany has, of course, been the substantial rise in personal taxation which has accompanied the unification of East and West.

In the future, growth in most Western European countries is likely to be fostered by

Reproduced by permission of the OECD

Economic recovery in most Western European countries is now firmly established, following a prolonged period of tentative growth

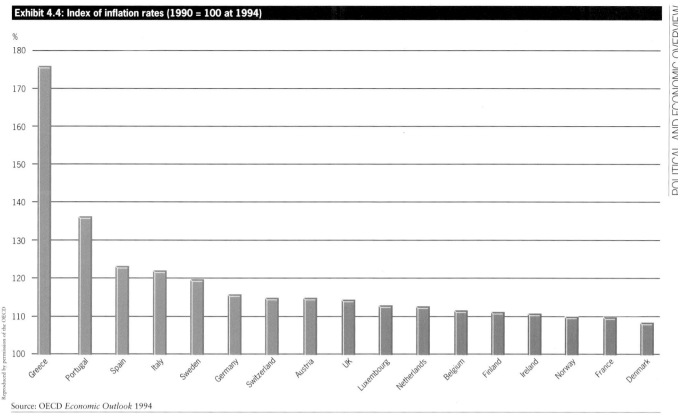

Exhibit 4.4: Index of inflation rates (1990 = 100 at 1994)

Source: OECD *Economic Outlook* 1994

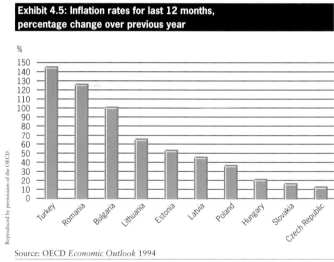

Exhibit 4.5: Inflation rates for last 12 months, percentage change over previous year

Source: OECD *Economic Outlook* 1994

Exhibit 4.6: Inflation in Central and Eastern Europe – percentage increase in average level of consumer prices over previous year

	1993	1994	1995	1996
Bulgaria	64	120	60	30
Czech Republic	21	11	9	7
Hungary	23	20	17	12
Poland	35	30	23	18
Romania	295	130	45	35
Russia	885	250	125	42
Slovakia	23	16	12	8

Source: OECD *Economic Outlook* 1994

broader based recovery, increasing personal consumption and rising levels of business investment to meet growing domestic demand. Export performance is also expected to remain strong in the medium term.

In Central and Eastern Europe, those countries that have led the way in structural adjustment (for example Poland, Hungary and the Czech Republic) are likely to reap the benefits of their earlier investment in equipment, machinery and public construction projects. In addition, private consumption in these countries has contributed to buoyant domestic demand to the extent that measures have been taken by governments in several countries to dampen consumer spending through the introduction of wage controls and value-added tax.

After recession – inflation

As continental Europe emerges from recession and enters into a period of economic growth,

inflation is projected to rise. It is likely to remain at reasonably low levels, however, and will stay fairly stable in Western Europe. In Italy and Sweden, for instance, the combination of recession, lower wage settlements and cyclical productivity gains has ensured a disinflationary environment. Nevertheless, as wages grow and productivity increases slow, the domestic cost climate is likely to worsen.

In Central and Eastern Europe, meanwhile, high inflation levels will continue in the medium term, although significant improvements are forecast (see Exhibit 4.6).

Wage levels

Compensation levels per employee in business have increased in all European countries since 1990, as Exhibit 4.7 illustrates. In Eastern Europe, real wages have been rising and have therefore helped to increase levels of consumer spending power.

The pattern of rising wages is set to change, however: OECD projections indicate that increases in compensation levels will fall from 1993 levels in the majority of European countries (in some cases sharply, for example in Greece, Portugal, Spain and Sweden) by 1996. Likely exceptions to this trend are France, Italy, Austria, Denmark, Finland, Norway and Switzerland.

Countries such as Hungary, Poland and the Czech Republic are likely to reap the benefits of their earlier investment in machinery

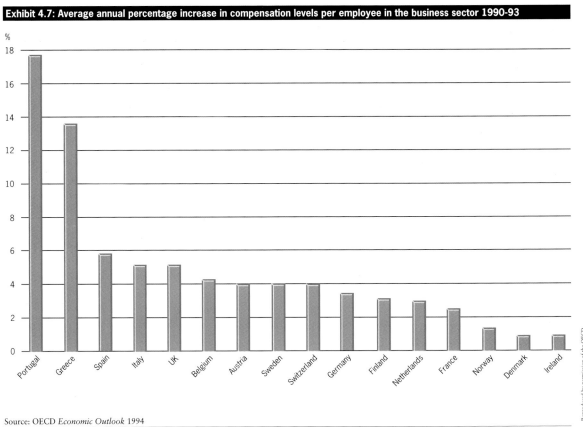

Exhibit 4.7: Average annual percentage increase in compensation levels per employee in the business sector 1990-93

Source: OECD *Economic Outlook* 1994

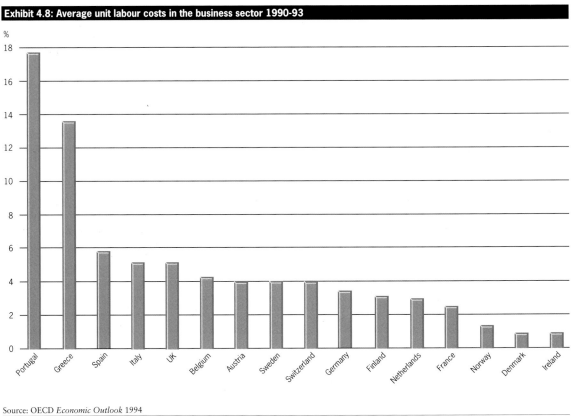

Exhibit 4.8: Average unit labour costs in the business sector 1990-93

Source: OECD *Economic Outlook* 1994

Employment levels in most EEA states are likely to rise, reversing the downward trend seen since 1990

Unit costs

Unit labour costs in the business sector have risen in European countries since 1990, although rates of change have varied considerably (as Exhibit 4.8 illustrates).

Rates of change in Greece and Portugal, for example, have been notably higher than in other West European countries, particularly Denmark, Ireland and Norway.

Employment: gains and losses

Employment levels in most EEA states are likely to rise, reversing the downward trend seen since 1990. Overall, employment gains have been modest across Europe (weaker than in the US or Japan), though sectoral and national improvements have occurred. For example, employment levels in Italy have risen strongly since the second quarter of 1994, and full-time employment has

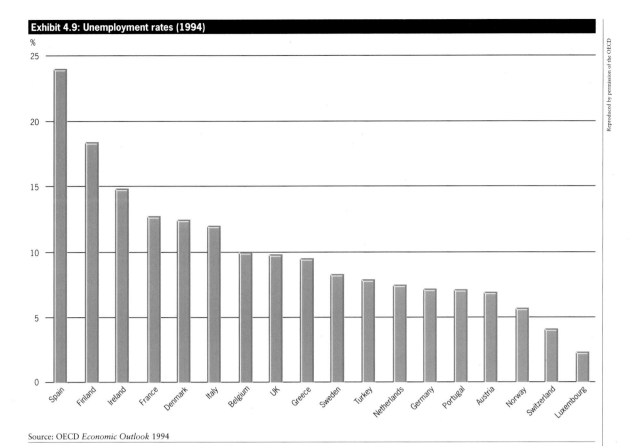

Exhibit 4.9: Unemployment rates (1994)

Source: OECD *Economic Outlook* 1994

Exhibit 4.10: Percentage registered unemployed – Central and Eastern Europe

	1993	1994	1995	1996
Bulgaria	16.3	17.0	17.0	17.0
Czech Republic	3.5	3.5	4.0	4.5
Hungary	12.1	10.8	11.5	11.0
Poland	15.7	16.5	16.0	15.0
Romania	10.2	11.0	12.0	12.5
Russia	5.7	9.0	12.0	14.0
Slovakia	14.4	15.0	13.0	11.0

Source: OECD *Economic Outlook* 1994

also begun to recover in the UK. Employment growth has returned to Spain, where the level of unemployment has on average been far higher than in other European countries (peaking at around 24 per cent). Growth in manufacturing employment has taken place in Germany, where strong export demand has helped to boost the demand for manufactured goods.

Exhibit 4.11: Dun & Bradstreet country risk indicator

Denmark	1b	Czech Republic	3a
Switzerland	1b	Poland	3b
Austria	1c	Slovenia	3b
Belgium	1c	Turkey	3b
France	1c	Hungary	3c
Germany	1c	Slovak Republic	4b
Ireland	1c	Estonia	5a
Luxembourg	1c	Latvia	5a
Netherlands	1c	Lithuania	5a
Norway	1c	Romania	5a
UK	1c	Bulgaria	5b
Finland	1d	Albania	5c
Italy	1d	Croatia	5d
Sweden	1d	Belarus	6a
Portugal	2a	Russia	6d
Spain	2a	Ukraine	6d
Greece	2c		

Source: Dun & Bradstreet *International Risk and Payment Review*

In Central and Eastern Europe, registered unemployment rates vary considerably, from approximately 3 per cent in the Czech Republic to more than 16 per cent in Poland. Continuing strong export performance in the region may help to offset employment losses caused by post-communist restructuring.

Exhibit 4.9 charts recent unemployment rates. The current overall trend is positive, with only Italy, Greece, Portugal, Iceland and Spain among those Western countries expected to suffer rising levels of unemployment in the medium term to 1996. Unemployment across the Western European region will be around 11 per cent through 1995, representing approximately 21-22 million people. For most Eastern European countries, the OECD projects that unemployment levels will rise by 1996, but only to a limited extent (see Exhibit 4.10).

The relative risks

For many companies looking to invest in a new region or country, political and economic risk is a key concern. Particularly in Eastern Europe, changes in the political and economic environment have occurred at different speeds and to varying degrees. In terms of risk, this leads to a wider divergence between East and West European countries.

Exhibit 4.11 provides an indication of how European countries are assessed with regard to risk. It is based on a scoring system that goes from one to seven: one indicates a relatively risk-free environment for investment, while seven indicates an extremely risky environment. Scores also run from A to D, thus 1A is a better risk than 1D, and so on. It is interesting to note that in terms of risk, the fastest-developing Eastern European economies are now almost on a par with some Western economies.

In terms of risk, the fastest developing Eastern economies are almost on a part with some Western economies

33

Chapter 5

LABOUR

Labour is one of the most important issues to consider in the location decision-making process. Once the courting by the development agencies has died down and the final grant payment has been made, the standard of a company's workforce is likely to be a major factor in the ongoing profitability of any operation.

As with most other location factors, labour issues are considered at a number of stages in the decision-making process. During the early stages, regions will no doubt be included or dismissed on the basis of their labour record – an initial selection process which is often based on personal experience or that of colleagues, or on media images, all which maybe negative or out of date.

Companies and development agencies alike should be wary of being misled by this intuitive process, as by the time 'on the ground' evaluation is undertaken, potentially suitable locations may have been struck off the agenda for no more reason than a bad press report five or six years ago. It is, moreover, difficult to go back on such a position once it has become established in the search evaluation. For example, the UK's industrial relations record has improved to the extent that in some recent years, Germany has lost more working days due to strikes – and yet the UK's past poor record still features at the forefront of many company executives' minds when they are formulating their location requirements.

Labour issues, probably more than any other, are extremely hard to assess in a purely objective manner. Many of the problems of information collection and assessment discussed in Chapter 3 also apply here, and the situation is further complicated by the fact that human factors are involved. Much tends to rely on the 'feel' of a particular area – something that is determined specifically by the individual or individuals undertaking the analysis, the organisational culture of the investing company and the function/nature of the facility.

In considering employment matters, firms seek to answer a number of key questions, including:
● Will the appropriate workforce be available in the number and skills required?
● How much will the workforce cost (in wages, statutory on-costs and customary local benefits)?
● How productive are the workers?
● Are the terms and conditions of work flexible?

Where overseas staff need to be recruited, the attractiveness of the location to, and the cost of, expatriates also needs to be considered.

Labour availability: a key concern
The availability of labour, especially skilled labour, is often more important than cost, though the two are usually inter-related. A low-cost location which cannot provide the appropriate skill levels may lead to considerable resources being spent on training, on recruitment from elsewhere and on moving employees from other parts of an organisation.

The analysis of labour force availability requires an understanding of both supply and

The standard of a company's workforce is likely to be a major factor in the ongoing profitability of an operation

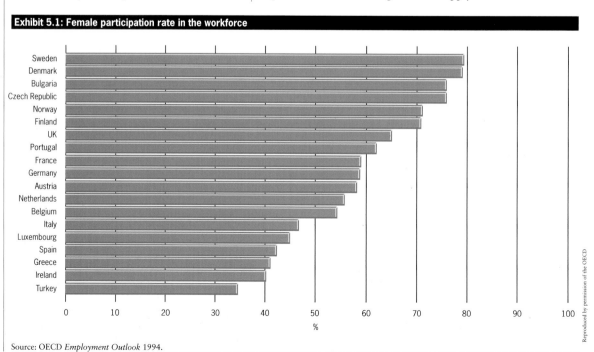

Exhibit 5.1: Female participation rate in the workforce

Sweden, Denmark, Bulgaria, Czech Republic, Norway, Finland, UK, Portugal, France, Germany, Austria, Netherlands, Belgium, Italy, Luxembourg, Spain, Greece, Ireland, Turkey

%

Source: OECD *Employment Outlook* 1994.

Exhibit 5.2: Average unemployment, 1991-93 (EU12=100)

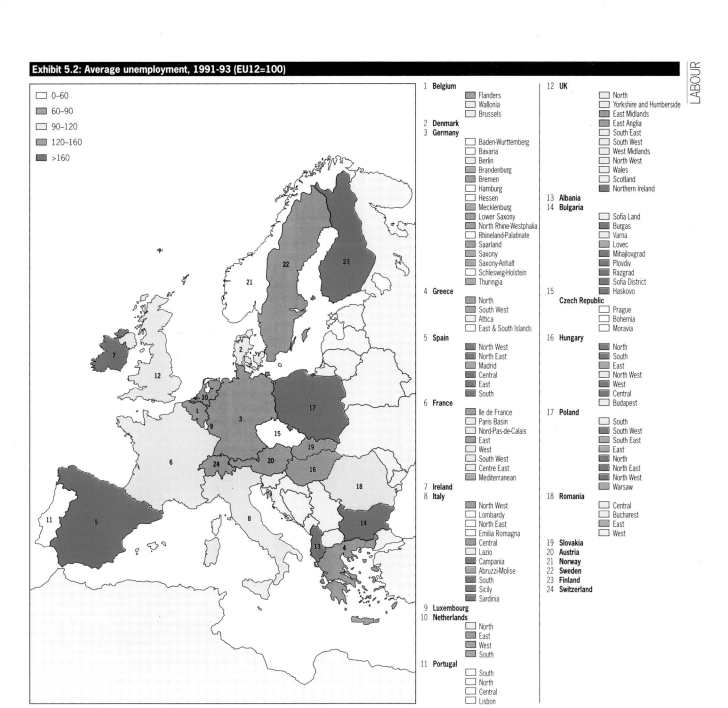

Legend:
- ☐ 0–60
- ▨ 60–90
- ☐ 90–120
- ▨ 120–160
- ■ >160

1 **Belgium**
- Flanders
- Wallonia
- Brussels

2 **Denmark**
3 **Germany**
- Baden-Wurttemberg
- Bavaria
- Berlin
- Brandenburg
- Bremen
- Hamburg
- Hessen
- Mecklenburg
- Lower Saxony
- North Rhine-Westphalia
- Rhineland-Palatinate
- Saarland
- Saxony
- Saxony-Anhalt
- Schleswig-Holstein
- Thuringia

4 **Greece**
- North
- South West
- Attica
- East & South Islands

5 **Spain**
- North West
- North East
- Madrid
- Central
- East
- South

6 **France**
- Ile de France
- Paris Basin
- Nord-Pas-de-Calais
- East
- West
- South West
- Centre East
- Mediterranean

7 **Ireland**
8 **Italy**
- North West
- Lombardy
- North East
- Emilia Romagna
- Central
- Lazio
- Campania
- Abruzzi-Molise
- South
- Sicily
- Sardinia

9 **Luxembourg**
10 **Netherlands**
- North
- East
- West
- South

11 **Portugal**
- South
- North
- Central
- Lisbon

12 **UK**
- North
- Yorkshire and Humberside
- East Midlands
- East Anglia
- South East
- South West
- West Midlands
- North West
- Wales
- Scotland
- Northern Ireland

13 **Albania**
14 **Bulgaria**
- Sofia Land
- Burgas
- Varna
- Lovec
- Mihajlovgrad
- Plovdiv
- Razgrad
- Sofia District
- Haskovo

15 **Czech Republic**
- Prague
- Bohemia
- Moravia

16 **Hungary**
- North
- South
- East
- North West
- West
- Central
- Budapest

17 **Poland**
- South
- South West
- South East
- East
- North
- North East
- North West
- Warsaw

18 **Romania**
- Central
- Bucharest
- East
- West

19 **Slovakia**
20 **Austria**
21 **Norway**
22 **Sweden**
23 **Finland**
24 **Switzerland**

demand for specific skill sets. To define their labour needs, companies must consider not just the number of workers required (and the timeframe over which they will be required), but also the characteristics they are looking for in the workforce. This will be driven by the project's objectives and the organisation's strategy. Many relocations are caused by – and prove to be the stimulus for – major changes in labour force practices. Some companies see relocation as a chance to get rid of 'dead wood' and introduce new working practices.

The main factors which impact on labour availability include:
- Size of population in a given region and, more importantly, the available workforce;
- The level of female participation within the available workforce;
- Unemployment levels in the area.

Population and available workforce
During the 1980s, the size of the available labour force has risen by nearly 1 per cent a year within the European Union. The extent to which this will continue depends on:
- Continuing net inward migration (from 1985 to 1992 net inflow into the EU exceeded 5 million; this has been to a large extent responsible for the particularly sharp increases in the available workforce);
- Continuing life-expectancy improvements;
- An end to the slowdown of, and a possible increase in, fertility rates;
- The degree of participation of the population in the available workforce, and in particular continuing increases in female participation.

The EU forecasts that its labour force is likely to continue growing at its previous high rate due to continuing immigration and growing female participation. However, there will be major regional and national differences.

In the former communist countries, the recent major economic and structural changes have led in some cases to a decrease in population and high outward migration. Of greatest concern is

Some companies see relocation as a chance to get rid of 'dead wood' and introduce new working practices

35

Exhibit 5.3: GDP per person employed 1993 (EU12=100)

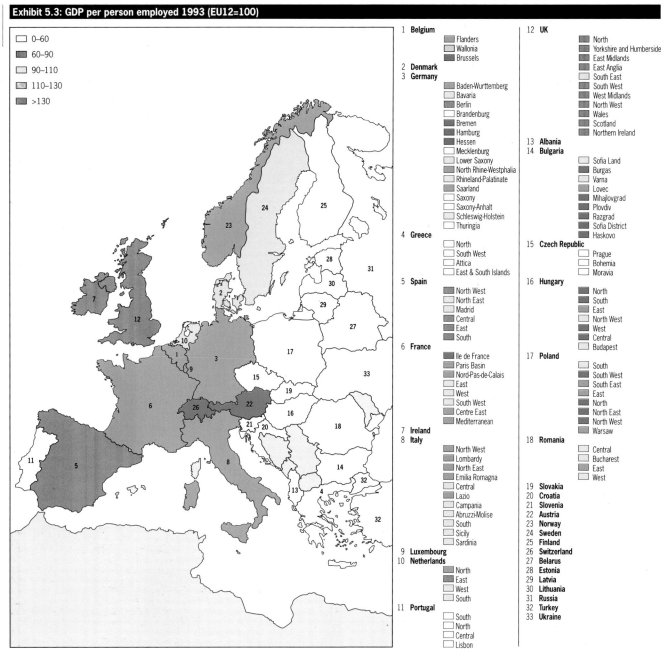

Legend:
- ☐ 0–60
- ☐ 60–90
- ☐ 90–110
- ☐ 110–130
- ☐ >130

1 **Belgium**
- Flanders
- Wallonia
- Brussels

2 **Denmark**

3 **Germany**
- Baden-Wurttemberg
- Bavaria
- Berlin
- Brandenburg
- Bremen
- Hamburg
- Hessen
- Mecklenburg
- Lower Saxony
- North Rhine-Westphalia
- Rhineland-Palatinate
- Saarland
- Saxony
- Saxony-Anhalt
- Schleswig-Holstein
- Thuringia

4 **Greece**
- North
- South West
- Attica
- East & South Islands

5 **Spain**
- North West
- North East
- Madrid
- Central
- East
- South

6 **France**
- Ile de France
- Paris Basin
- Nord-Pas-de-Calais
- East
- West
- South West
- Centre East
- Mediterranean

7 **Ireland**

8 **Italy**
- North West
- Lombardy
- North East
- Emilia Romagna
- Central
- Lazio
- Campania
- Abruzzi-Molise
- South
- Sicily
- Sardinia

9 **Luxembourg**

10 **Netherlands**
- North
- East
- West
- South

11 **Portugal**
- South
- North
- Central
- Lisbon

12 **UK**
- North
- Yorkshire and Humberside
- East Midlands
- East Anglia
- South East
- South West
- West Midlands
- North West
- Wales
- Scotland
- Northern Ireland

13 **Albania**

14 **Bulgaria**
- Sofia Land
- Burgas
- Varna
- Lovec
- Mihajlovgrad
- Plovdiv
- Razgrad
- Sofia District
- Haskovo

15 **Czech Republic**
- Prague
- Bohemia
- Moravia

16 **Hungary**
- North
- South
- East
- North West
- West
- Central
- Budapest

17 **Poland**
- South
- South West
- South East
- East
- North
- North East
- North West
- Warsaw

18 **Romania**
- Central
- Bucharest
- East
- West

19 **Slovakia**
20 **Croatia**
21 **Slovenia**
22 **Austria**
23 **Norway**
24 **Sweden**
25 **Finland**
26 **Switzerland**
27 **Belarus**
28 **Estonia**
29 **Latvia**
30 **Lithuania**
31 **Russia**
32 **Turkey**
33 **Ukraine**

In 2010, most EU countries will have more people aged over 40 than under

the fact that those who do leave are the highly skilled, resulting in a lack of such individuals in the workforce.

In most of western Germany and in parts of northern Italy and Greece, the labour force is likely to decline in size. In Belgium, eastern Germany, Denmark and the UK, it is expected to remain stable, while growing rapidly in Spain, parts of Portugal, France and the Netherlands. Turkey has one of the fastest growing populations: by 2025 it is expected to be the second most populous country in Europe after Russia.

In the longer term, the picture is less clear. The ageing of the population is likely to continue: in the year 2010, the immediate post-war 'baby boom' generation will be over 65, and most EU countries will have more people aged over 40 than under.

Despite this ageing factor, the available workforce may increase if rising female participation and other factors, such as immigration, continue to feature. What this means, however, is that while the labour force increases, its composition will change from young male to older female employees. This will have major implications for the kind of working environment and hours that employers will have to provide.

The changing nature of work is also an important factor in the demand for employees. As heavy industry, which predominantly employed males, is replaced by a service sector economy where interpersonal skills are more important, demand for female workers will rise while declining for males.

The female factor

As demand for female labour increases, a low level of female participation may indicate a potentially large untapped workforce. Eastern Europe and Scandinavia, for example, have historically had very high female participation rates of 70-80 per cent, while those in Southern Europe are generally far lower (see Exhibit 5.1).

It should be noted that the level of male participation in the European workforce currently ranges from 75-90 per cent. The ratio of

Exhibit 5.4: Manufacturing labour costs 1994

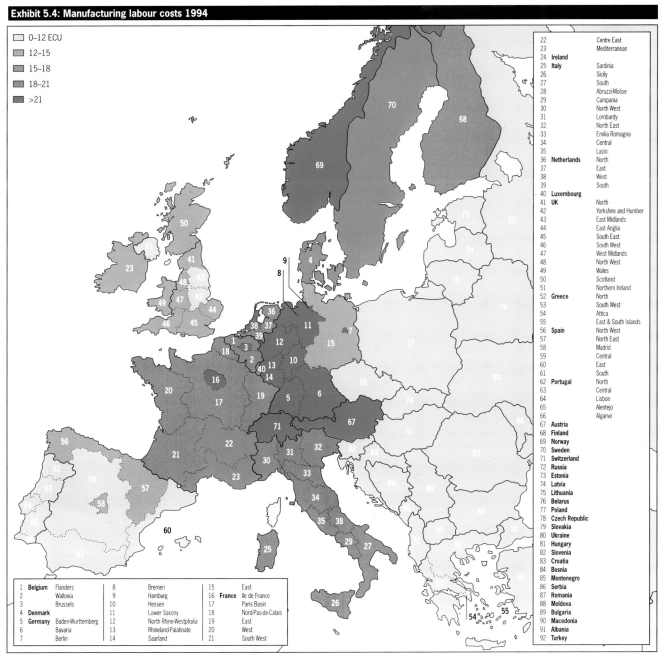

- 0–12 ECU
- 12–15
- 15–18
- 18–21
- >21

22		Centre East
23		Mediterranean
24	Ireland	
25	Italy	Sardinia
26		Sicily
27		South
28		Abruzzi-Molise
29		Campania
30		North West
31		Lombardy
32		North East
33		Emilia Romagna
34		Central
35		Lazio
36	Netherlands	North
37		East
38		West
39		South
40	Luxembourg	
41	UK	North
42		Yorkshire and Humber
43		East Midlands
44		East Anglia
45		South East
46		South West
47		West Midlands
48		North West
49		Wales
50		Scotland
51		Northern Ireland
52	Greece	North
53		South West
54		Attica
55		East & South Islands
56	Spain	North West
57		North East
58		Madrid
59		Central
60		East
61		South
62	Portugal	North
63		Central
64		Lisbon
65		Alentejo
66		Algarve
67	Austria	
68	Finland	
69	Norway	
70	Sweden	
71	Switzerland	
72	Russia	
73	Estonia	
74	Latvia	
75	Lithuania	
76	Belarus	
77	Poland	
78	Czech Republic	
79	Slovakia	
80	Ukraine	
81	Hungary	
82	Slovenia	
83	Croatia	
84	Bosnia	
85	Montenegro	
86	Serbia	
87	Romania	
88	Moldova	
89	Bulgaria	
90	Macedonia	
91	Albania	
92	Turkey	

1	**Belgium**	Flanders	8		Bremen	15		East
2		Wallonia	9		Hamburg	16	**France**	Ile de France
3		Brussels	10		Hessen	17		Paris Basin
4	**Denmark**		11		Lower Saxony	18		Nord-Pas-de-Calais
5	**Germany**	Baden-Wurttemberg	12		North Rhine-Westphalia	19		East
6		Bavaria	13		Rhineland-Palatinate	20		West
7		Berlin	14		Saarland	21		South West

women to men ranges from 1:1.03 in Hungary (where women make up almost half of the workforce) to 1:2.48 in Turkey.

Rates of unemployment

A more immediate indicator of available labour is the local unemployment rate. This is particularly relevant if the requirement is for relatively unskilled workers, who generally make up the majority of the unemployed at all stages of the economic cycle.

Unemployment in Europe is well in excess of 20 million, or around 10 per cent of the workforce. A regional breakdown of unemployment is shown in Exhibit 5.2; as local unemployment rates can fluctuate significantly over a short time period, the average rate for 1991-93 has been used. The exhibit clearly illustrates that there are large variations between regions.

Unemployment levels have been highest in Spain and southern Italy, Ireland, Northern Ireland and the new German Länder. In Central and Eastern Europe, meanwhile, rates vary con-

siderably from very low levels in Russia (often hiding high levels of under-employment) to very high levels in Albania and parts of Poland.

Even in these times of high unemployment, there are some regions – especially in western Germany and northern Italy – which have a relatively tight labour market.

In using unemployment as an indicator of labour availability, it is necessary to look behind the headline figure and consider 'who are the unemployed?' It is important to understand their age and skill composition as well as their geographical concentration and the nature of their former employers. The unemployed can be an excellent source of available skills, but care needs to be taken to match specific company requirements to the pool of labour.

Companies relocating to, and within, Europe should have little difficulty in accessing a general supply of labour, except perhaps in those regions, characterised by low working population growth and low unemployment levels, where there is a tight labour market.

As heavy industry is replaced by a service sector economy where interpersonal skills are more important, demand for female workers will rise

Exhibit 5.5: Hourly compensation costs for manufacturing workers

	US$	Index US=100
US	16.73	100
Japan	19.01	114
Austria	20.27	121
Belgium	21.21	127
Denmark	19.12	114
Finland	16.56	99
France	16.23	97
Germany*	25.71	154
Greece**	7.46	43
Ireland	12.18	73
Italy	15.99	96
Luxembourg***	17.9	107
Netherlands	19.95	119
Norway	20.21	121
Portugal	4.6	27
Spain	11.5	69
Sweden	17.7	106
Switzerland	22.63	135
UK	12.76	76

* Former West Germany only. ** 1992 figure. *** 1991 figure.

Source: US Department of Labor, 1994

As well as considering the broad indicators outlined above, companies should also seek to:
● Understand the local industrial structure and the profile of local companies;
● Identify major employers and recent investors;
● Establish the extent of skill shortages and difficulty of recruitment;
● Assess the level of competition for skills in the locality now and in the future;
● Evaluate the local education and training capacity.

The failure to investigate and understand the implication of these labour characteristics adequately can have a major impact on the cost and effectiveness of a new operation. This can be just as true of small-scale operations as major projects with significant labour requirements.

Labour costs

Wage costs are a major business expense and are driven by the general availability of labour, availability of specific skills and local expectations as well as the company's remuneration policy.

In addition to the basic salary paid to individuals, companies have to bear a variety of additional costs which include statutory obligations and benefits negotiated through union/collective agreements and local practices. These additional costs, borne by the employer, can amount to more than 45 per cent of gross salary, and in some cases an employee's net 'take home' pay may be less than half the total wage cost.

However, a high level of additional contributions does not necessarily entail a higher overall labour cost. In those countries where state contributions are low, employers may have to pay more in direct salaries to enable employees to obtain goods and services which elsewhere are provided by the state.

Exhibit 5.5 (above) shows, in absolute terms, the hourly compensation costs for production workers in manufacturing, taking account of both earnings and fringe benefits and statutory social cost add-ons, for 1993. Figures for the US and Japan are included for comparative purposes. While several EEA countries have higher pro-

An employee's net 'take home' pay may be less than half the total wage cost

duction wage costs than the US, Finland, France and Italy are comparable. Wage costs in the UK, Ireland and Spain are appreciably lower, while in Greece and Portugal they are significantly lower. Wage rates in the countries of Eastern Europe are typically less than 20 per cent of those in the US.

Labour costs also differ between regions within the same country. This is most evident in the UK, while other countries with national collective agreements have less significant regional differences. Those differences that do exist tend to be due to the higher wages paid in the major cities.

The question of productivity

The disadvantages of high labour costs can be offset by higher productivity, and conversely the advantage of low labour costs can be lost by poor productivity.

Comparison of workforce productivity is, however, particularly difficult. The main measure, and one which is readily available, is output (i.e. gross domestic product, or GDP) per employee. It is important, though, to recognise that output differences reflect not just the skills and efforts of the workforce, but also the combined influence of a number of factors, such as industrial structure, new technology, capital investment, capacity utilisation, energy use and managerial skills.

There are significant differences in output per employee across Europe (as Exhibit 5.3 shows). Output levels are highest in western Germany, northern Italy, Switzerland and Austria. The comparative performance of Eastern and Central Europe and Turkey is well below that of the worst performing European Union regions. Over the next few years, however, the best performing areas of Eastern Europe are likely to start overtaking regions in Portugal and Greece in terms of output per employee.

The flexibility of the workforce

Consideration should also be given to labour flexibility – that is, willingness to work shifts, do overtime and adapt to various work practices. This flexibility will depend on the individuals concerned, on local customs and on management practices which operate within a labour regulation framework made up of statute (including case law), collective agreements and trade union influence.

Labour practices throughout Europe

Although European integration and the social dimension have been important in a number of labour areas – such as the lifting of the ban in many countries on female night work – the concept of subsidiarity has ensured that diversity of labour practices throughout Europe continues.

Terms and conditions of employment

In most countries, the terms and conditions of employment are set out in a hierarchy of laws which are enhanced by national or local collective agreements. Collective agreements are, in most European countries, legally binding and enforceable. Legislation usually lays down the requirement for a contract of employment and limits the use of fixed-term contracts. It also determines general standards of working conditions, such as maximum working hours and restrictions on night work, time off, dismissals and procedures for individual and collective redundancies.

Over the next few years, the best performing areas of Eastern Europe are likely to start overtaking regions in Portugal and Greece in terms of output per employee

Exhibit 5.6: Working hours/overtime arrangements

	Normal weekly working hours	Maximum working hours per week	Maximum overtime	Normal pay premium for overtime work*
Austria	38.5	40	65 hrs p.a.	50
Belgium	38	40	65 hrs per 3 months	50
Denmark**	37	–	–	50
Finland	37.5	40	20 hrs per 2-week period	50
France	39	39	130 hrs p.a.	25
Germany	37	40	60 hrs p.a.	25
Greece	40	40	150 hrs p.a.	25
Ireland	39	48	240 hrs p.a.	50
Italy	39	40	–	25
Luxembourg	n/a	40	2 hrs per day	n/a
Netherlands	38	48	12 hrs per week	25
Norway	37.5	40	200 hrs p.a.	40
Portugal	41	44	160 hrs p.a.	75
Spain	40	40	80 hrs p.a.	75
Sweden	40	40	200 hrs p.a.	80
Switzerland	41.6	50	350 hrs p.a.	25
UK**	39	–	–	25

* Pay premium calculated for a hypothetical two hours' overtime as a percentage of pay for a normal hour of work. ** In Denmark and the UK there are no general regulations on working hours.

Source: OECD *Employment Outlook/Income Data Services Contracts and Terms and Conditions of Employment* 1994

In certain circumstances it is possible to obtain exemptions from these provisions, either through collective agreement, by permission of local employment offices or through the company's trade union. Such exemptions will not typically apply to senior management posts.

Statute and collective agreements together set sector-related maximum working week and overtime restrictions in many countries. Local negotiations can also lift the more burdensome overtime restrictions. An indication of overtime rates/hours is given in Exhibit 5.6 (above).

In many countries, women and young persons have generally not been permitted to work at nights. Following a European Court of Justice ruling in 1991, however, the European Commission has undertaken proceedings against countries still upholding such a ban against women, though night work for children is still forbidden and for adolescents it remains severely restricted.

In 1993, an EU directive specified a normal maximum working week of 48 hours (including overtime) to be averaged over four months, or longer if a collective agreement exists (some sectors – for example transport and sea fishing – are excluded). This directive was to be implemented by November 1996 but, to accommodate UK interests, an extension to 2003 has been allowed.

Sunday and public holiday working is restricted in most European countries, but again, exemptions apply, especially in continuous manufacturing processes.

Exhibit 5.7 (below) shows the average number of hours worked per year by country. As can be seen, there are significant variations. Ireland and Portugal work the greatest number of hours: the Irish work 30 per cent more hours than the Swedes, who work the shortest hours.

The distribution of hours worked, as opposed to the average, illustrates interesting differences across Europe. With the exception of the UK, most countries have a heavy concentration of employees working within a narrow range of hours. In Spain, for example, some 70 per cent of employees usually work 40 hours per week; in Italy and Ireland the figure is 48 per cent.

Average annual leave and public holidays in each country is shown in Exhibit 5.9. Public holidays vary, since within countries there may also be a number of local or regional holidays in addition to any national holidays. Exhibit 5.9

With the exception of the UK, most countries have a heavy concentration of employees working within a narrow range of hours

Exhibit 5.7: Average annual hours worked, 1993 or 1994

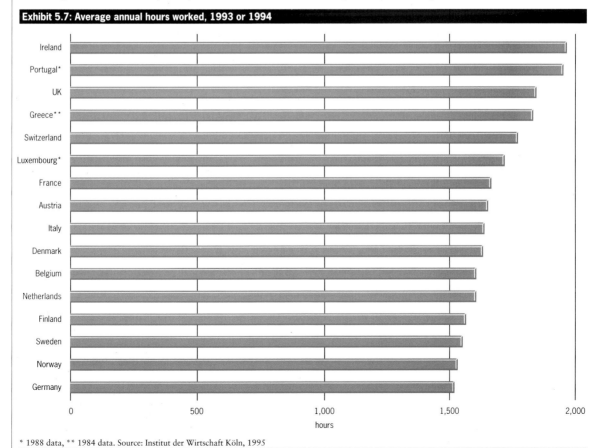

* 1988 data, ** 1984 data. Source: Institut der Wirtschaft Köln, 1995

Ireland and Portugal work the greatest number of hours: the Irish work 30 per cent more hours than the Swedes

Exhibit 5.8: Employees' total weekly hours (employees usually working less than 16, or more than 48, hours per week)

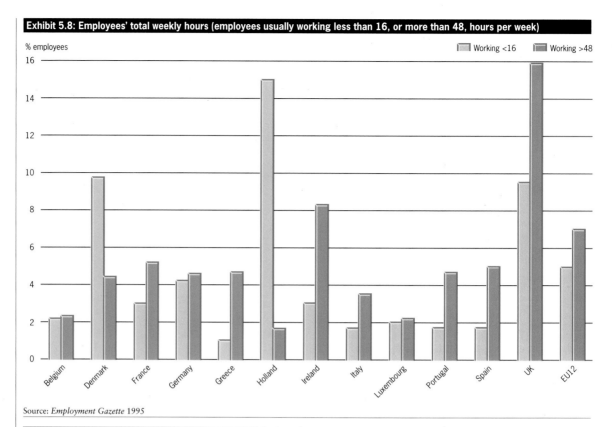

Source: *Employment Gazette* 1995

Reproduced by permission of the OECD

Part-time employment is becoming more embedded in working practices and is no longer concentrated in retailing

Exhibit 5.9: Annual leave and public holidays, 1994

Country	Annual leave (days)	Public holidays
Austria	26.5	10.5
Belgium	20	11
Czech Republic	15	10
Denmark	25	7
Finland	37.5	6
France	25	10
Germany	30	10
Greece	22	9
Hungary	20-30	8
Ireland	21	9
Italy	35	7
Netherlands	32.5	7
Norway	21	7
Poland	14-26	10
Portugal	22	14
Spain	24	14
Sweden	25	7
Switzerland	23.8	9
Turkey	10-20	11.5
UK	25	8

Source: Institut der Deutschen Wirtschaft Köln, 1995

Exhibit 5.10: Percentage in part-time employment

	All employees	Female employees
Austria	9.1	20.5
Belgium	11.8	27.4
Denmark	23.1	37.8
Finland	7.9	10.4
France	12.9	24.5
Germany	15.5	34.3
Greece	3.9	7.2
Ireland	8.4	17.8
Italy	5.4	10.5
Luxembourg	7.5	17
Netherlands	32.8	44.6
Norway	26.9	47.1
Spain	7.2	11
Switzerland	24.3	41.3
UK	23.2	44.6

Source: OECD *Employment Outlook* 1994

therefore includes customary holidays which employees are not expected to work, even though they may not actually be statutory holidays.

Maternity and paternity leave should also be taken into account by companies assessing different countries/locations. An EU directive gives pregnant women an automatic right to 14 weeks' leave, during which maintenance of pay (or an allowance, which is usually a combination of statutory benefit and company contributions) must be paid. Paternity leave has not been agreed at a European level, but a number of countries, including Switzerland and the Netherlands, have instituted paternity leave entitlements.

Part-time employment has increased, though there are notable variations in its use between countries (Exhibit 5.10). In the Netherlands, part-time employment has almost doubled in the 10 years to 1992 to 33 per cent of the total working population, while in Norway it has remained static at 27 per cent. It is becoming more embedded into working practices and is no longer concentrated in retailing, though part-time posts are still, predominantly, filled by female workers.

The use of fixed-term employment contracts (i.e. employment ending on a specified date) is increasing across Europe (Exhibit 5.11). This practice is influenced by the economic climate, and by technological change, and is often used by companies to circumvent employment protection legislation. Fixed-term employment is highest in Greece, Portugal and Spain, and is concentrated in the service and agricultural sectors. Collective agreements have, however, limited its use in the manual/industrial sectors.

The regulation of fixed-term contracts varies considerably between countries, especially in relation to its duration, renewal, compensation and 'requirement of reason', and is summarised in Exhibit 5.12. The maximum duration of fixed-term contracts has gradually been increased across a number of countries including Germany.

The maximum duration of fixed-term contracts has gradually been increased across a number of countries

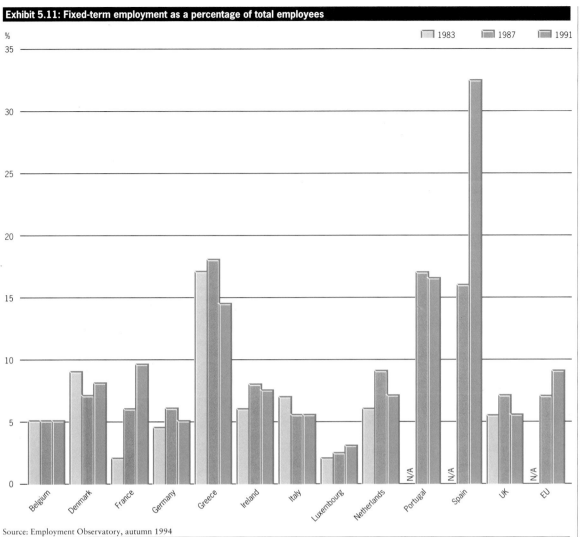

Exhibit 5.11: Fixed-term employment as a percentage of total employees

☐ 1983 ☐ 1987 ☐ 1991

Source: Employment Observatory, autumn 1994

Dismissal, other than for redundancy, has to be for a 'just cause'

Conditions on the use of fixed-term contracts are particularly strict in Italy, while in Finland, France, Germany, Greece, Norway and Sweden they are limited to specific cases such as seasonal and temporary work. The scope for renewal of such contracts also differs from country to country, with the Netherlands, Denmark, Ireland and the UK having no specific regulations.

All European countries have some form of minimum wage system or restrictions set by national legislation and/or collective agreements. National statutory minimum wages apply in France, Greece, the Netherlands and Portugal. In most Scandinavian countries, Germany, Italy and Belgium it is collective agreements that set the minimum (these can be extended to firms in the same sector who have not fully participated in the negotiation process). In Denmark, meanwhile, wages are set by collective agreement but cannot be extended to other firms in the same sector but outside the agreement. The UK only sets a statutory minimum wage for agricultural workers, while in Ireland there is no statutory minimum wage, though restrictions are set by joint labour committees for some industries.

Dismissal and redundancy

Dismissal, other than for redundancy, has to be for a 'just cause', and the works council, where one exists, is usually informed. If the relevant procedures are not correctly followed, the dismissal is illegal and the worker concerned will be entitled to compensation. (Exhibit 5.13 provides a guide to the length of notice required in each country before an employer can terminate a contract of employment.)

In most instances, the length of notice required depends on the length of time an employee has served, and also, in some cases, his or her age. These requirements are often backed up by collective agreements. Immediate dismissal is, however, allowable in cases of gross misconduct.

Notice periods vary from country to country. In the UK, for example, notice entitlement is only one week for the first two years' of service; in Switzerland, it is seven days in the probationary period and one month for the first year; in Germany, a minimum of one month's notice is advisable after two years' service; and in France it is one month for between six months, and two years' service.

In cases of redundancy, workers who have completed the required length of service are usually entitled to severance pay. The definition of redundancy differs according to country, but in small- and medium-sized enterprises it is generally based on a percentage of the workforce (10-30 per cent) affected within a specified period (three to nine months); in larger firms it is based on an absolute number of workers. Severance pay usually ranges from one week's to one month's pay for every year of service, up to a maximum, usually of one year's pay. Once again collective agreements may increase these provisions.

Exhibit 5.12: Regulations for fixed-term contracts in the European Union, 1994

	Belgium	Denmark	France	Germany	Greece	Ireland
Requirement of reason	No	No	10 reasons, including seasonal work, replacement and temporary nature of work	7 categories of reasons under case law, including seasonal work, replacement and temporary nature of work	4 reasons, including temporary nature of work	No
Duration	Maximum duration of 2 years for replacement contracts	No maximum or minimum duration	Maximum duration varies between 9 months and 2 years, according to reason for fixed term	Statutory maximum for fixed-term contracts under the Employment Promotion Act normally 18 months; (24 in exceptional cases)	No maximum or minimum duration	No maximu or minimum duration contracts,
Renewal	In a limited number of industries and under particular circumstances, such as temporary increase in workload	Unlimited	Once, up to maximum fixed term	In general, only up to the maximum fixed term; 4 months' interruption before a new contract can be concluded under the Employment Promotion Act	Twice	Unlimited
Automatic conversion into permanent contract	Yes, if continued after the contractual or maximum fixed term and in case of illegality	Yes, if found to be illegal	Yes, if continued after the contractual or maximum fixed term	Yes, if continued after the contractual or maximum fixed term and in case of illegality	Yes, if continued after the contractual or maximum fixed term	No
Compensation at the end of the fixed term	No. Employer pays twice the normal rate of compensation if dismissal before the expiry of the fixed term was unlawful	No	Yes, except in cases of seasonal work	Compensation is 6 per cent of the overall gross wage	No	No

Source: Schomann/Rogowski/Kruppe 1994

There are broad geographical bands of labour legislation across Europe... The UK stands out as the least regulated labour market

In a number of European countries, the process of redundancy can be extremely bureaucratic. A company's trade union or works council (and possibly the local employment office too) will all have the right to suggest an alternative course of action which may be preferable to redundancy. And in many cases, a period of notice cannot be served on the employee in question until the employer has received official authorisation.

Exhibit 5.13: Period of notice required for termination of employment

	All employees	White collar	Blue collar
Austria	1/2-5 months	14 days	
Belgium		3-6 months	7-56 days
Denmark		1-6 months	21-70 days
Finland	1 month		
France	1-2 months		
Germany	4 weeks-7 months		
Greece	1-6 months		
Ireland		1-8 weeks	3-6 months*
Italy		1-6 months	15 days-4 months
Luxembourg	2-6 months		
Netherlands	1-26 weeks		
Norway	1-6 months		
Portugal	60 days		
Spain	1-3 months		
Sweden	2-6 months		
Switzerland	1-3 months		
UK	1-12 weeks		

* Executives. Source: Income Data Services/IPD 1995

Works councils

In the majority of countries, there are mandatory systems for the establishment and rights of works councils (see Exhibit 5.14), though their role differs greatly within individual companies. The number of employees forms the basis on which works councils are established: in Austria and Germany, for example, employees in an establishment of more than five staff can form a works council which is entitled to mandatory representation on the management board. In Belgium and Luxembourg, the figures are 100 and 150 respectively, while the European average is around 50.

Works councils generally have the right to consultation over matters such as dismissal and redundancy, and they can influence terms and conditions of employment. Legislation often requires that they should be informed of company proposals affecting the workforce and that provision should be made for them to put forward alternative proposals.

An EU directive under the Social Chapter requires that multinational companies with more than 1,000 employees in total and more than 100 in at least two member states must establish a European works council in order to promote the flow of information and the consultation of employees. (The United Kingdom, however, has opted out of this provision.)

In summary there are broad geographical bands of labour regulation across Europe. The

There are many areas of employment legislation that are becoming more flexible

Italy	Luxembourg	Netherlands	Portugal	Spain	United Kingdom
9 reasons, including seasonal work, replacement, and temporary and occasional character of work	10 reasons, including seasonal work, replacement and occasional character of work	No	No, unless the fixed term is for less than 6 months. In this case the work must be temporary in nature	11 reasons, including specific purposes, but excluding seasonal work	No
Maximum fixed term six months; in case of training	Maximum fixed term 2 years	No maximum or minimum years with the possibility of renewal for a further 3 years)	Maximum duration 6 years (maximum fixed term is 3	Maximum fixed term 3 years	No maximum or minimum
Once, for the same duration as the previous contract	Twice, up to the maximum fixed term	Unlimited	Up to the maximum fixed-term	Up to the maximum fixed term	Unlimited
Yes, if continued after the contractual or maximum fixed term	Yes, if continued after the contractual or maximum fixed term	No; automatic renewal for a maximum of 1 year if continued for the first time after expiry of the fixed term. Conversion into a permanent contract if continued beyond the extra year without explicit renewal	Yes, if continued after the maximum fixed term	Yes, in cases of illegality less than a more than	Yes, if the fixed-term contract is concluded for month and lasts 3 months
No	No	No	Yes, 2 days' basic remuneration for each month of service	No	No

EU directives will place a veneer of similarity across a growing number of countries

Exhibit 5.14: Form and role of employee representation in the workplace

Country	Compulsory presence of union delegates	Compulsory presence of works council*	Mandatory representation on management board	Co-determination rights of employees' representative bodies
Austria	No	Yes (>5)	Yes	Heavy involvement in local working condition matters
Belgium	No	Yes (>100)	No	Definition of general criteria for dismissals and working conditions
Denmark	No	Yes (>35)	Yes	Definition of local working conditions
Finland	No	Yes (>30)	Yes	Definition of local working conditions; right to delay employers' decision to contract out
France	Yes (>50)	Yes (>50)	Yes	Elaboration of social plan in case of collective dismissals
Germany	No	Yes (>5)	Yes	Definition of recruitment procedures; local working conditions; collective dismissals
Greece	Yes (>50)	Yes (>50)	Yes (>50)	Co-determination rights in local working condition matters only if the trade union agrees (in practice, very unusual)
Ireland	No	No	No	No regulations except for Joint Labour Committees
Italy	No	No	No	No regulations
Netherlands	No	Yes (>35)		Definition of recruitment procedures, local working conditions, dismissal policy
Norway	Yes	Yes		Definition of local working conditions
Portugal	Yes	Compulsory	No	Limited role
Spain	Optional	Optional	No	Limited role
Sweden	Yes	Yes		Extended rights; priority right of interpretation in co-determination matters
Switzerland	No	No	No	Limited role
UK	No	No	No	Limited role

Source: OECD *Employment Outlook* 1994. *Shows minimum no. of staff needed for presence of works council to be compulsory

Mediterranean countries along with Sweden have the highest levels of regulation, followed by Germany and France. The rest of Europe forms a core middle banding, with the UK standing out as the least regulated labour market.

There are many areas of employment regulation that are becoming more flexible, while at the same time EU directives will place a veneer of similarity across a growing number of countries.

Trade unions and collective agreements
The level of union representation – which in general has been declining – is obviously of interest to employers. The density of unions varies greatly

Exhibit 5.15: Trade union density and collective bargaining coverage rates

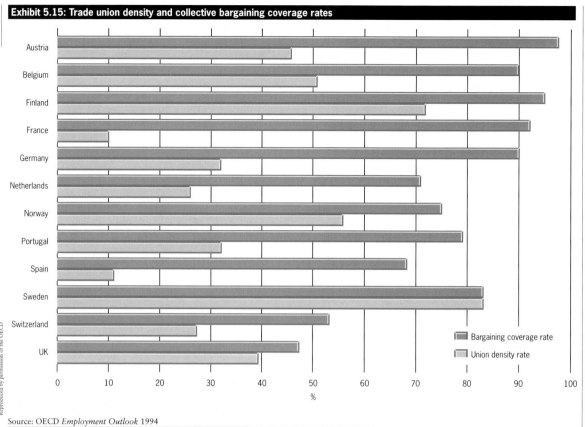

Bargaining coverage rate
Union density rate

Source: OECD *Employment Outlook* 1994

The
Netherlands,
Germany and
Austria have
had an
excellent
industrial
relations
record

Exhibit 5.16: Industrial disputes – average working days lost per 1,000 employees per year in all industries and services 1989-93

	Average 1989-93
Austria	10
Belarus	16
Belgium	30*
Denmark	30
Finland	170
France	30
Germany (FDR)	20
Greece	470
Hungary	2*
Ireland	160*
Italy	250*
Moldova	403*
Netherlands	20
Norway	60
Poland	49*
Portugal	60
Russia	16
Spain	430
Sweden	70
Switzerland	<1
Turkey	400
Ukraine	50
UK	70

* Indicates average based on incomplete data
Source: International Labour Organisation, 1995

In terms of
strike action,
Italy, Spain
and in
particular
Greece have
the worst
records

trade union density – such as France, at 11 per cent – are now placed in a more equal position with regard to the relative proportion of the workforce covered by collective agreements.

In some countries, the institutional framework of collective bargaining has been an incentive to join unions, while in others (such as France and Spain, where collective agreements do not discriminate in favour of union members and agreements are widely applied), it is a disincentive.

The practice of extending collective agreements to cover firms which operate in the same sector but which have not been directly involved in the negotiations is common in Austria, France, Belgium and Portugal; it is limited in Finland, Germany, Netherlands, Spain and Switzerland, and is negligible in Sweden, Norway and the UK.

Exhibit 5.16 shows the average number of working days lost due to strike action between 1987-91 in different European countries. It is worth noting that high union membership is not necessarily related to troubled industrial relations. Spain, for instance, fares badly, even though it has a low trade union density.

When comparing countries, it is important to remember that there are significant differences in the methods of calculation. In the UK, there is no compulsory notification of strikes but indirectly affected workers are included in data, while in Germany the opposite is the case. Common to both the UK and Germany, meanwhile, is the inclusion of strikes where they affect 10 or more workers. And France excludes civil-service stoppages from its statistics. What is clear, however, is that the Netherlands, Germany and Austria have all had an excellent record (though recent disputes in Germany have tarnished that country's image). Italy, Spain and, in particular, Greece have the worst records.

across Europe, ranging from 10 per cent in France and 11 per cent in Spain to 83 per cent in Sweden (Exhibit 5.15).

Of equal importance from the point of view of flexibility is the coverage of collective bargaining agreements. The extent of collective agreement has become more uniform across Europe: countries which fare well on the headline indicator of

EDUCATION AND TRAINING

Chapter 6

Low-cost countries such as India now produce vast numbers of well-trained graduates

The availability of a suitably qualified workforce is a key location requirement for most companies. Before any location decision is taken, it is essential to ensure that the local workforce has all the skills necessary to undertake the tasks that will be required. Failure to do so can result in problems – as has been demonstrated by the experiences of a number of electronics companies which have been attracted to low-wage locations in Southern Europe only to find that, once there, they cannot recruit staff with the right skills. These companies have been forced either to employ staff from other countries, often at considerable expense, or bring in trainers from the parent company to teach new recruits.

A country's comparative advantage often depends on the skills offered by its management and labour. It's for this reason that we see a growing emphasis, especially in European countries, on raising educational standards and skill levels. Increasingly, there is a global market for labour. At the moment this affects mainly unskilled workers: component production or assembly work that requires only unskilled labour can be undertaken in a developing country where wage costs are low. And since low-cost countries such as India now produce vast numbers of well-trained graduates, many tasks requiring a high level of skill – computer software development or pharmaceutical R&D, for instance – are also being transferred away from high-cost Western economies. Thanks to modern telecommunications, many administrative functions, such as data entry or claims processing, can also be undertaken in lower-cost locations.

Basic literacy and numeracy skills are taken for granted in most European countries. Even so, there is concern in certain countries that school-leavers, though able to read and write at a basic level, do not have sufficient skills to follow written instructions or process numerical data such as order forms. In one OECD country, for example, it is estimated that:
- 7 per cent of adults are unable to read;
- 9 per cent are generally unable to follow any but the most simple written instructions;
- 22 per cent can only follow very simple written instructions;
- 62 per cent are classed as functionally literate, that is, they can follow and interpret most written instructions.

While one might expect that it is the older members of the workforce who have the greatest difficulties with literacy, in fact the study found that 20 per cent of 25- to 34-year-olds were classed as functionally illiterate. There is no reason to expect that the situation is markedly different in other European countries, and as

companies' skill requirements increase, it must be cause for concern that 20-30 per cent of the workforce are in danger of becoming unemployable.

There are, however, considerable variations in educational standards throughout Europe. These are due in part to the diversity of education and training on offer and are generally of a national rather than regional nature. Exhibit 6.1 sets out the varying compulsory education requirements in different European countries.

Long degree courses and the requirement to do some form of national service mean that the age at which new graduates start work can vary from 21 in the UK and Ireland to 27 or 28 in Germany and Switzerland. However, with the end of the

Exhibit 6.1: Duration of compulsory education

	From (age)	To (age)	Duration (years)	Typical university graduation age	National service
Albania	6	13	7		√
Austria	6	15 (17)	9 (11)	23	√
Belarus	6	17	11		√
Belgium	6	16 (18)	10 (12)	22	X
Bulgaria	6	16	10		√
Croatia	7	15	8		√
Czech Republic	6	16	10		√
Denmark	6/7	16/17	9	22	√
Estonia	7	15	8		√
Finland	7	17	10	23	√
France	6	16	10	21	√
Germany	6	16 (18)	10 (12)	25	√
Greece	5½	14½	9		√
Hungary	6	16	10		√
Ireland	6	15	9	21	X
Italy	6	14	8	22	√
Latvia	7	15	8		√
Lithuania	7	15	8		√
Luxembourg	6	15	9	23	X
Macedonia	7	15	8		√
Moldova	6	17	11		√
Netherlands	5	16	11	22	√
Norway	7	16	9	22	√
Poland	7	14	7		√
Portugal	6	14	8	22	√
Romania	6	14	8		√
Russia	6	17	11		√
Slovakia	6	16	10		√
Slovenia	7	15	8		√
Spain	6	14 (16)	8 (10)	21	√
Sweden	7	16	9	23	√
Switzerland	6/7	15/16	8/9	26	√
Turkey	7	15	8	23	√
Ukraine	6	17	11		√
UK	5	16	11	21	X

(Figures in brackets include compulsory part-time education for those not enrolled in full-time education).

Source: OECD, *Education in OECD Countries 1993*/UNESCO *Statistical Yearbook 1994*

Reproduced by permission of the OECD

Exhibit 6.2: Percentage of each age group enrolled in full-time education, 1992

Age	17	18	19	20	21	22	23	24
	%	%	%	%	%	%	%	%
Belgium	91	75	60	44	31	20	12	7
Czech Republic	39	17	14	12	12	10	1	1
Denmark	74	69	53	41	35	31	26	24
Finland	85	82	40	36	40	40	33	27
France	85	78	65	47	34	26	16	10
Germany*	82	83	61	41	31	37	19	18
Hungary	45	18	14	13	10	8	5	3
Ireland	77	58	39	30	19	11	6	6
Netherlands	75	73	62	49	39	28	22	16
Norway	87	78	69	37	33	30	26	4
Poland	82	51	31	23	15	13	11	8
Portugal	49	42	31	26	16	11	8	7
Spain	67	54	45	43	34	28	19	14
Sweden	87	61	24	17	16	16	14	13
Switzerland	78	75	53	30	21	17	15	12
Turkey	32	26	18	15	9	7	6	4
UK	57	34	24	20	14	8	5	4
US	74	54	42	33	28	20	13	8

* Western Germany only. Source: OECD, *Education at a Glance* 1995

Cold War and the increasing sophistication of modern weaponry, conscription is likely to be considerably reduced. Belgium has, in fact, already decided to abolish national service in 1995.

Despite the increasing importance placed on education and training, there is still a wide variation in enrolment rates in post-compulsory education (see Exhibit 6.2). For example, more than a quarter of the population aged 24 in Finland are still in full-time education, whereas in Hungary only 17 per cent of 18-year-olds remain in full-time education. However, account should be taken of part-time courses, which are popular in countries such as the UK.

When it comes to entry into tertiary education, Europe tends on average to come a long way behind the US and Japan, as Exhibit 6.4 shows. In recent years, however, the economic recession in Europe has led to a marked increase in the numbers of young people staying on in education rather than trying to join the labour market.

Indicators of educational attainment are limited to the levels achieved by those people now in work. In many Southern European countries, a

Exhibit 6.3: Percentage of the population aged 25-64 by highest level of education undertaken (1991)

	Primary	Lower secondary	Upper secondary	Tertiary Total	(non univ.)	(univ.)
US	7	10	47	36	(13)	(24)
Norway	0	21	54	25	(12)	(12)
Sweden	0	33	44	23	(11)	(12)
Germany	0	18	60	22	(11)	(11)
Switzerland	0	19	60	20	(13)	(7)
Belgium	28	29	24	20	(10)	(10)
Netherlands	18	26	37	20	(13)	(6)
Denmark	0	39	43	18	(6)	(13)
Finland	0	40	42	18	(8)	(10)
Ireland	33	27	24	16	(8)	(8)
UK	0	35	49	16	(7)	(10)
France	23	27	35	15	(5)	(10)
Former Czechoslovakia	0	27	63	10	(0)	(10)
Spain	63	15	12	10	(0)	(10)
Austria	0	33	61	7	(0)	(7)
Turkey	74	9	11	6	(0)	(6)
Italy	39	33	22	6	(0)	(6)
Portugal	88	5	3	4	(1)	(3)

Figures may not add up due to rounding. Source: OECD, *Education at a Glance* 1993

Exhibit 6.4: Ratios of entry into full-time tertiary education, 1991

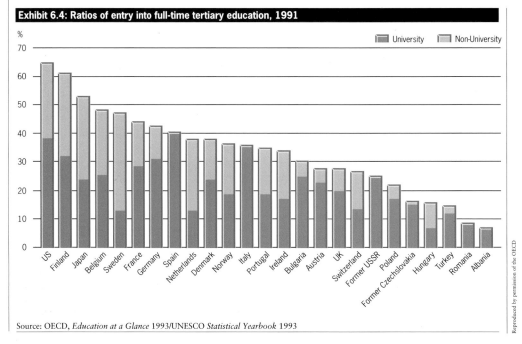

Source: OECD, *Education at a Glance* 1993/UNESCO *Statistical Yearbook* 1993

When it comes to tertiary education, Europe tends to come a long way behind the US and Japan

Surveys
continue
to highlight
shortages
of engineers
and skilled
computer
staff across
Europe

Exhibit 6.5: Percentage of undergraduates studying selected subjects

	Mathematics & computer science	Engineering
Austria	6.1	9.8
Belgium	3.6	11.5
Denmark	3.7	14.7
Finland	6.7	21.5
Germany	4.9	18.8
Greece	3.6	18.4
Ireland	3.0	13.2
Italy	3.2	9.5
Netherlands	0.7	6.1
Norway	0.6	11.9
Spain	4.0	10.0
Sweden	5.6	18.6
Switzerland	2.1	15.2
Turkey	2.1	13.2
UK	5.0	15.3

Source: OECD, *Education at a Glance*, 1993

Exhibit 6.6: Public expenditure on labour markets training and participation rates, 1993

	% of GDP	% of the labour force assisted
Sweden	0.83	3.1
Germany	0.55	2.3
Ireland	0.48	3.4
Finland	0.46	2.5
Denmark	0.42	7.7
France	0.39	5.0
Norway	0.37	3.5
Portugal	0.25	5.3
Belgium	0.23	7.8
Netherlands	0.19	1.6
Greece	0.15	1.2
UK	0.14	0.9
Spain	0.12	1.9
Hungary	0.11	1.2
Austria	0.10	1.3
Switzerland	0.03	3.1
Slovak Republic	0.03	1.1
Poland	0.03	0.4
Italy	0.02	n/a
Bulgaria	0.01	0.5
Czech Republic	0.01	0.2

Source: *Employment Outlook*, OECD 1994

very high percentage of the population have attained only primary-school education (though this applies mostly to the older generation).

Surveys continue to highlight shortages of engineers and skilled computer staff across Europe. It is interesting to note the percentage of undergraduates reading those subjects: they seem relatively unpopular in countries like the Netherlands and Italy, whereas in Finland over a quarter of undergraduates study them (Exhibit 6.5).

The importance of training
A cynical view of publicly funded training schemes is that they are a way of taking jobless people off the unemployment register. Indeed, the increased attention given to training coincided with a rise in youth unemployment in the 1980s. However, training schemes that are hastily introduced for political reasons rarely improve the quality of vocational education.

In general, governments spend most of their training resources on the unemployed, though in Denmark and Portugal more employed than unemployed people are assisted.

The infrastructure for training
The training infrastructure in any region depends on a country's attitude to public sector support. In the UK, for example, there is a network of training providers which are government-led but firmly placed within the private sector. Training and Enterprise Councils in England and Wales, and Local Enterprise Companies in Scotland distribute the largest part of government training and development budgets, but their boards and top management are primarily drawn from the local business community, and they are empowered to develop schemes and programmes to suit local requirements. Participation in these schemes is voluntary, as is companies' financial contribution to them. In contrast, companies in France are required to spend a set proportion of income on training (currently 1.5 per cent of the pay bill). If this is not done, firms must pay a compulsory levy to a central fund which is used for independent training provision.

Where membership of a chamber of commerce is mandatory for trading companies, as in France, the chambers are sufficiently large and well funded to play a major role in training provision. Where membership is voluntary, however, chambers of commerce tend to lack the funding needed to provide significant training.

A company looking to locate to a region will need to take a close look at local skills in the context of its needs both now and in the future. These skills – and their costs – will vary from country to country. In Switzerland, for example, a highly educated and skilled workforce is available but labour costs there are relatively high, whereas in Ireland substantial amounts have been spent on education and training without adding significantly to labour costs.

Skill availability also varies across sectors. If a region is strong in particular sectors, the skill base will reflect those strengths. It is possible, of course, that firms established in the location already employ the full regional complement, so new entrants will need either to poach those workers, at a premium, or train others from scratch.

Where education stops and training begins
Belgium
In Belgian schools, from the age of 14 pupils choose between a transition stream, where the priority is to prepare them for higher education, and a qualification stream, which provides a technical and vocational education. This reflects a trend in many EU member states for a clear divide between so-called academic education and vocational training. It is a divide that is now resisted, however, as we see greater emphasis being placed on the need to match educational provision to the demands of industry and commerce, and on making further educational establishments more aware of industrial requirements.

Denmark
Vocational training programmes can last up to eight years, with 80 weeks out of that time spent at college. Most courses last between three and four years. Companies are required to pay a subsidy which is used to finance the training schools. The type of training provided is greatly determined by trade committees which operate as employer-union bodies and decide the training courses and their contents at each training centre.

Training
schemes that
are hastily
introduced
for political
reasons
rarely
improve the
quality of
vocational
education

France
Vocational training includes apprenticeships, training credits and sandwich courses. Apprenticeships last up to three years and can lead to a vocational baccalaureate. Training credits are available to people aged between 16 and 25 who are without qualifications and who wish to undertake training leading to a vocational qualification. French employers are required to pay a training tax, but expenditure on training is deductible from the tax. Consultation about training programmes is compulsory at both industry and company level. Companies must produce an annual training plan each year and consult their works councils on its content.

Negotiations at industry level between unions and management bodies take place at least every five years and cover:
● The type of training schemes in operation;
● Programmes for young people;
● Training for those with few/no qualifications;
● Equality for men and women;
● Training for employees of small firms.

Discussions at company level take place several times a year and focus on particular features of training such as: funding; technology; work organisation; content of courses.

By law, employees who have worked for a firm for more than a year are allowed up to one year's full-time training, with pay, outside the company.

Germany
Pupils can leave full-time education at the age of 16, but they must continue vocational training either at a specialist craft college or part-time, as part of a sandwich course. This so-called 'dual system' has been praised throughout Europe as an example of training that recognises industry's needs while at the same time being fully complementary to the main educational system. Because it has developed out of the network of trade associations and guilds which are a particular feature of German industry, attempts at transplanting this system to other countries have, however, had mixed results.

The central feature of Germany's dual system is the combination of on-the-job training by qualified employees and off-the-job training in special vocational schools. The provision of training places is entirely a choice for the employer and there is no state compulsion or tax reward for training. However, the high proportion of German firms which undertake this kind of training reflects the widespread belief that it is essential to a company's success. Moreover, because labour mobility is relatively low in Germany, companies can be confident that investment in training is likely to produce tangible benefits.

Criticisms of the dual system principally concern the lengthy period needed for basic skills to be learned, and the scheme's general inflexibility. But for most people, the comprehensiveness of the system and its ability to allow the academically less gifted to acquire qualifications outweigh any disadvantages.

Though training provision is voluntary, German employers are required to give their staff paid leave for education. Companies are also required to discuss training arrangements with unions. The cost of training is fully borne by employers, and though there are no mandatory levies or taxes, certain trades require by law the employment of experienced staff.

Ireland
Vocational training is administered and co-ordinated by An Foras Aiseanna Saothair (FAS), which is financed through a levy on firms and by a state grant. Companies are not required by law to provide training, but FAS has the power to call on particular industrial sectors to create training strategies. FAS is developing a common apprenticeship programme for Ireland which will replace the current haphazard combination of different qualifications and methods.

Italy
In Italy, the main complaint concerning vocational training is the lack of a common system for certification and qualification. The education system is seen as separate to vocational training, and there is little contact or co-ordination.

This lack of a clear vocational training infrastructure has led to some trade associations creating training centres. A number of major employers have also developed their own arrangements. One example is ENFAPI, an independent training body funded by Fiat, Pirelli, Zanussi, IBM Italia and Montedison.

There are no compulsory levies in Italy nor legal dictates on the level of training a firm should maintain, but employees do have some statutory rights regarding time off for training.

The Netherlands
Most post-school vocational training is carried out by Senior Secondary Vocational Colleges (MBOs) and lasts three to four years. MBO training offers four options:
● Engineering and technology, including laboratory and maritime education;
● Economics and administration, covering trade and commerce, textiles, catering and tourism;
● Social services and healthcare;
● Agriculture, including forestry, food technology.

There are no legal obligations on Dutch firms to release for training employees who are above the age of 18. However, a number of collective agreements prevail specifying entitlements to levels of training and study leave. Though no compulsory funding requirements are imposed on firms, there is an increasing tendency for unions to negotiate training packages in collective agreements.

Spain
Vocational training is co-ordinated by the state, with overall control from a tripartite body consisting of representatives from trade unions, employers and government. Young people aged between 16 and 20 can be employed on a fixed-contract trainee basis, with 25-50 per cent of their time spent in training. There is a scale of assistance to employers towards the wages of trainees, dependent on the mix of training and productive activity. A separate scheme exists for companies prepared to employ trained women in sectors where they are under-represented.

An interesting variation to national schemes prevails in the Basque region, where the employees' confederation CONFEBASK has established on-the-job training designed around specific skill shortages and provided by skilled workers.

Germany's 'dual system' has been praised throughout Europe as an example of training that recognises industry's needs

ACCESS TO MARKETS

The first edition of *Regions of the New Europe* looked forward to the creation of the Single European Market. The second considered the likely impact of the establishment of the European Economic Area and the reunification of Germany. This edition is written at a time of further enlargement of the European Union and increasing investments and trade between Eastern, Central and Western Europe. All these developments have taken place over a period of just five years, changing completely the notion of the 'European Market'.

Inward investment within Europe, principally from the US and the Far East, has also led to an increase in intra-European trade. This is because, in most cases, the incoming operations are centralised in a small number of locations – perhaps a single location – from which the entire European market is served. Similarly, many domestic European companies have begun to reorganise their operations on a pan-European basis, with facilities in different states specialising in complementary operations and supplying either groups of nations or the whole of the European Free Trade Area. In many instances, this has resulted in increased production efficiencies due to reduced duplication, though at the cost of a growing logistics burden.

Chapter 7

While the growth in cross-border trade has provided significant opportunities for many companies, it has also brought threats in the form of heightened competition. Consumers have been quick to capitalise on this fact and are demanding higher standards of product and service quality. The result has been not only an emphasis on total quality, shorter product life-cycles and product flexibility (often manifested as a demand for a large number of product variants), but also on lower costs and ever better customer service levels, backed up by near-perfect information and administration.

Effective logistics management has thus become a key to survival and success: transport and inventory costs have to be minimised while customer service levels must be maintained across a much larger marketplace. As leading companies have rationalised themselves on a pan-European basis, reorganising in line with supply-chain principles, they have had to pay particular attention to market accessibility when choosing their operating locations.

Market accessibility: the essential issues

Market accessibility is the level of ease with which companies within a certain region can gain access to the main markets of Europe – that is, the areas where the greatest economic activity takes place. Market access is twofold: it involves being able to obtain not only the resources needed to carry out business, but also a place in which a company can sell its products, services, information or influence.

Although quality of transport and information infrastructure has an impact on market accessibility, distance is the most significant factor and this is, of course, determined by geography. Essentially, the more peripheral a region is, the greater the difficulty in accessing the main markets. A peripheral location may be a particular disadvantage to companies which:
● Have a significant proportion of their sales costs accounted for by land transport;
● Serve markets demanding very high customer service levels (particularly short lead times) and therefore cannot tolerate a great degree of uncertainty over supplies or transport without incurring a significant inventory penalty;
● Require proximity to the main centres of activity for reasons of maintaining influence;
● Need access to a wide variety of suppliers and services, or need to benefit from co-maker relationships (e.g. JIT arrangements) with suppliers who are concentrated near the main markets;
● Need access to a substantial market in order to obtain economies of large-scale production;
● Need rapid access to research or information which is concentrated at the economic centre;
● Need access to skilled or specialist staff who are attracted to the economic centre where opportunities are perceived to be greatest.

There are, however, circumstances in which companies may benefit from being located on the periphery or in intermediate areas between the centre and the periphery. These are firms which:
● Can offset the disadvantages of a peripheral location by the availability of low-cost labour;
● Need a stable workforce and low labour turnover and so require an environment where few other employers are competing for the workforce;
● Can attract the specialists they need because of the quality of life on offer;
● Serve a peripheral niche market away from the main suppliers;
● Require access to specialised skills which are concentrated in a peripheral region;
● Can benefit from lower congestion and, in some places, from a highly developed and underutilised infrastructure which has resulted from regional development programmes;
● Require access to natural resources not available at the centre;
● Can benefit from lower costs and greater availability of land and property and less restrictive planning constraints;
● Are sufficiently attracted by local or national grants, loans or incentives which outweigh the disadvantages of peripheral location.

Exhibit 7.1: Market accessibility 1995 (European average = 100)

Legend:
- <50
- 50–100
- 100–150
- >150

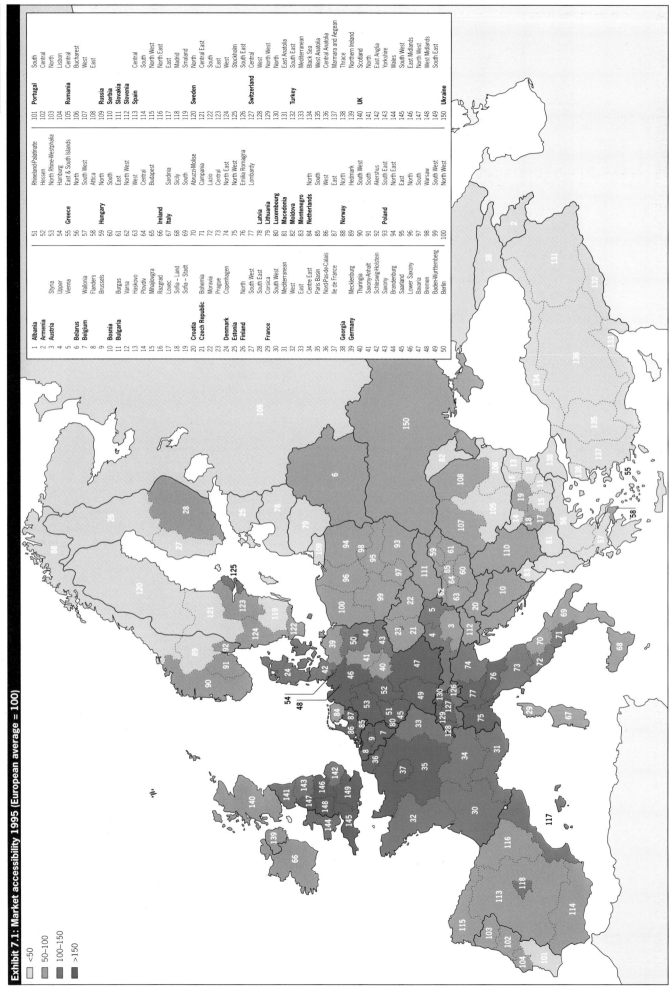

1	**Albania**		51	Rhineland-Palatinate	101	**Portugal**	South
2	**Armenia**		52	Hessen	102		Central
3	**Austria**	Styria	53	North Rhine-Westphalia	103		North
4		Upper	54	Hamburg	104		Lisbon
5		Vienna	55	East & South Islands	105	**Romania**	Central
6	**Belarus**		56	**Greece** North	106		Bucharest
7	**Belgium**	Wallonia	57	South West	107		West
8		Flanders	58	Attica	108		East
9		Brussels	59	**Hungary** North	109	**Russia** North
10	**Bosnia**		60	South	110	**Serbia**
11	**Bulgaria**	Burgas	61	East	111	**Slovakia**
12		Varna	62	North West	112	**Slovenia**
13		Haskovo	63	West	113	**Spain** Central
14		Plovdiv	64	Central	114	South
15		Mihajlovgra	65	Budapest	115	North West
16		Razgrad	66	**Ireland**	116	North East
17		Lovec	67	**Italy** Sardinia	117	East
18		Sofia – Land	68	Sicily	118	Madrid
19		Sofia – Stadt	69	South	119	Smaland
20	**Croatia**		70	Abruzzi-Molise	120	**Sweden** North
21	**Czech Republic**	Bohemia	71	Campania	121	Central East
22		Moravia	72	Lazio	122	South
23		Prague	73	Central	123	East
24	**Denmark**	Copenhagen	74	North East	124	West
25	**Estonia**		75	North West	125	Stockholm
26	**Finland**	North	76	Emilia Romagna	126	**Switzerland** South East
27		South West	77	Lombardy	127	Central
28		South East	78	**Latvia**	128	West
29		Corsica	79	**Lithuania**	129	North West
30	**France** South West	80	**Luxembourg**	130	North
31		South East	81	**Macedonia**	131	**Turkey** East Anatolia
32		West	82	**Moldova**	132	South East
33		Mediterranean	83	**Montenegro**	133	Mediterranean
34		East	84	**Netherlands** North	134	Black Sea
35		Centre East	85	South	135	West Anatolia
36		Paris Basin	86	West	136	Central Anatolia
37		Nord-Pas-de-Calais	87	East	137	Marmara and Aegean
38		Ile de France	88	**Norway** North	138	Thrace
39	**Georgia**		89	Hedmark	139	Northern Ireland
40	**Germany** Mecklenburg	90	South West	140	**UK** Scotland
41		Thuringia	91	South	141	North
42		Saxony-Anhalt	92	Akershus	142	East Anglia
43		Schleswig-Holstein	93	South East	143	Yorkshire
44		Saxony	94	**Poland** North East	144	Wales
45		Brandenburg	95	East	145	South West
46		Saarland	96	North	146	East Midlands
47		Lower Saxony	97	South	147	North West
48		Bavaria	98	Warsaw	148	West Midlands
49		Bremen	99	South West	149	South East
50		Baden-Wurttemberg	100	North West	150	**Ukraine**
		Berlin				

50

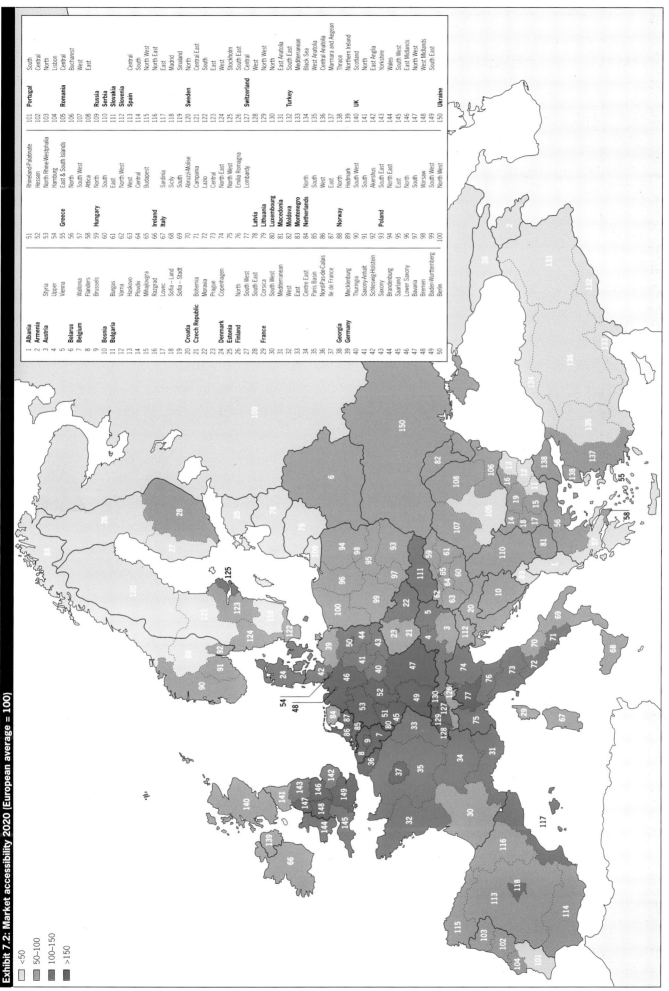

Exhibit 7.2: Market accessibility 2020 (European average = 100)

How regions compare

Ernst & Young has now developed its market accessibility index for the whole of Europe. Calculated following the method used in a 1988 EC study of peripheral locations and market accessibility, the index is based on the distance between each region and all other regions, weighted by the level of economic activity in the other regions measured by total output (and taking account of the need for sea crossings to reach some regions). Account has also been taken of each region's own demand relative to its surface area. An average level of accessibility has been calculated for the whole European Community and each region's accessibility is expressed as an index relative to that average. The results are shown in Exhibit 7.1.

We can see that there is a wide divergence in market accessibility across the different European regions. Those areas with the greatest market access are found in the so-called 'hot banana' or 'golden triangle' encompassing the south east of England, most of Benelux, northern France, the Rhine/Ruhr area of Germany, Switzerland and Lombardy. In addition, there are also a number of 'hot spots' which show a high degree of market accessibility because of their substantial local markets: these include Paris, Hamburg and Bremen.

What companies need to consider

We have already established that being in a peripheral location can be a benefit or a disadvantage for a company, depending on its operating characteristics. When making location decisions, it is therefore necessary to assess the likely impact of the peripheral location on a case-by-case basis. This is also true for other factors which may affect market accessibility. These include:

● Quality of road, rail and inland waterway infrastructure (Belgium, for example, has an excellent grid-iron motorway network and secondary road system, whereas Spain has a relatively poor internal road system);
● Degree of road congestion;
● Physical boundaries (such as the Pyrenees or the Alps);
● Political boundaries (Greece, for example, is separated from the rest of the European Union by countries currently experiencing civil war);
● Differential transport costs (labour, fuel and taxes are all relatively expensive in Germany, for instance);
● Remaining administrative barriers (such as the limited quota of permits for foreign commercial vehicles travelling to and from Central and Eastern Europe).

So, to give an example, although Lombardy in northern Italy has in general very good market accessibility, it would be an inappropriate location for an organisation that has a major part of its market in Germany, relies on road transport and is unable to obtain the necessary permits to cross Switzerland or Austria. Similarly, although it is geographically fairly peripheral, Catalonia (in north east Spain) may well prove to be an ideal location for a company providing specialist goods or services to towns and cities along the Mediterranean coast.

The view from Eastern Europe

For companies considering investing in Eastern Europe, physical access to markets may be a secondary issue compared with tariff and non-tariff barriers. Exhibit 7.3 summarises the situation in each country in the region.

Future developments

In general, tariffs are gradually being removed. However, the need to protect industries that are currently restructuring is likely to increase pressure for increased tariffs in certain sectors. (In addition, there are a number of possible future developments in technology, politics and infrastructure that are likely to have an impact on market accessibility, though in most cases the impact will be long- rather than short-term.)

The completion of further EU legislation and directives will continue to encourage growth in cross-border trade. Examples include the planned liberalisation of the road, rail and air transport markets. Progress towards monetary and political union within the EU will consolidate this growth. However, these processes are unlikely to change the current profile of market accessibility, and in fact it has been suggested that they will reinforce it, causing the peripheral regions to become even more isolated.

What will happen in the future, as the countries of Central and Eastern Europe become full market economies, and fast-growing economies such as Turkey become fully integrated into the rest of Europe? Based on the assumption that the majority of Eastern European economies will grow faster than those in the West, Exhibit 7.2 looks ahead 25 years and shows how the map of Europe might look like from a market access viewpoint in 2020.

Developments in transport infrastructure may have a modest effect on market accessibility in the short term. For example, the new fixed links connecting England to France and Copenhagen to the Danish mainland will reduce transportation costs and times for the UK and Denmark. The rest of Scandinavia should similarly benefit from a fixed link between Sweden and Denmark by the end of the century. In the longer term, if plans for a European integrated high-speed rail network and an integrated European air-traffic control system become a reality, the negative impact of distance on market accessibility will be considerably reduced generally across the continent. For those goods that can be easily transported by air, accessibility is already measured in distance from an international airport rather than to the final destination.

Looking ahead still further, it is argued that developments in the information and telecommunications infrastructure will reduce the requirement for business travel and transport. Together with an anticipated increase in congestion and pollution in the central regions, this could mean that future growth, encouraged by EU regional policy, will be focused on the periphery rather than central areas. However, this hypothesis depends on the acceptance of a dramatic change in business-related social behaviour and in the willingness of labour to move freely around the EU in search of employment. Changes of this scale are unlikely to occur quickly enough to have a significant effect on the distribution of economic activity in the short to medium term.

Exhibit 7.3: Trade regimes in Eastern Europe

Tariff and non-tariff import barriers	Export quotas and other export barriers	Exchange regime, other aspects
Albania		
Four rates of import tariffs from 0-30% ad valorem. No quantitative restrictions	Only eight product groups subject to export licences. Temporary export tax on six unprocessed natural-resource based products (introduced in March 1993)	Floating rate
Armenia		
Most goods tariff-free, except raw materials, equipment and some consumer goods. Maximum duty 20%. 10% general import tariff for non-FSU (former Soviet Union) countries. No quantitative restrictions except for health, national security or environmental reasons	No significant export taxes. Export licences for nine product groups. No quantitative restrictions	Floating rate
Azerbaijan		
Tariffs on imports from non-FSU countries eliminated. Import duties may be rendered ineffective by limited border controls	Strategic exports, mostly raw materials sold through bilateral state trading agreements at fixed prices. Extensive export quotas, licences and taxes	Official exchange rate, set basis of commercial bank rates. Strategic exports valued at domestic prices, creating multiple implicit exchanges rates
Belarus		
Import tariffs 10-20%, higher rates introduced in October 1993 for a few products, but FSU countries exempt. There are a few quantitative or licensing restrictions, mostly for health or national security	Export taxes of 2-30% since April 1992. 10% surcharge on convertible currency exports and barter outside the FSU since January 1993. Quota and licensing system for 11 product categories, mainly energy, raw materials and foodstuffs. Quantitative restrictions substantially reduced in early 1994	Floating rate with heavy central bank intervention. New rouble zone planned with Russia and Tadjikistan
Bulgaria		
22% average tariff on industrial goods reported in 1994. Restrictive import licences for a limited number of products. Some tariff quotas on processed foods and agricultural products	Export taxes on 30 items, mainly foodstuffs, have replaced most export quotas. Export quotas on six primary commodities. Occasional export bans on registration, and licensing restrictions still operative	Floating rate
Croatia		
10% import tax introduced in autumn 1993 as part of macroeconomic stabilisation programme. No quantitative restrictions.	High degree of liberalisation, most exports tariff-free	Floating rate with central bank intervention
Czech Republic		
Average weighted tariff 5.7% in 1993. Quantitative import restrictions on some agricultural products, textiles, clothing, steel and coal; licences for oil, gas and weapons	20% of exports required licensing in 1992. Export tax of 100% applies only to antiques and art works. Export licensing for livestock and plants, some natural resources and products such as textiles and steel which are subject to quotas in other countries	Peg to DM/US$
Estonia		
Only 14% of imports subject to duties; average weighted tariff 1.4% in 1993. Licences for alcohol and tobacco. No quantitative restrictions	Minimal barriers	Currency board with rate fixed to DM
Georgia		
2% uniform duty on all imports except food items. Import licences generally not required. No significant import quotas	8% tax on non-FSU exports. Significant licensing requirements	Interim currency, heavily restricted convertibility. Rate floating within these parameters
Hungary		
Approximately 10% of imports subject to quota or licensing restrictions, with number increasing in 1994. Average unweighted tariff 16%	Exports of fuels, wheat and industrial raw materials subject to licence. 80% of the agricultural budget in 1993 was devoted to export subsidies	Peg to US$/ECU basket
Latvia		
Basic tariffs 5-15% but many exceptions at 0.5% (raw materials, food products); some high agricultural tariffs	Export taxes on raw materials, precious metals and antiques. A few quantitative restrictions, mostly for health and national security reasons	Informal peg to SDR (Special Drawing Right)

Exhibit 7.3: Trade regimes in Eastern Europe

Tariff and non-tariff import barriers	Export quotas and other export barriers	Exchange regime, other aspects
Lithuania		
Import tariffs of 5-15%; higher for food products, alcohol and tobacco, and about a dozen manufactured goods (carrying tariffs of up to 25%)	Some export taxes on raw materials and foodstuffs. Some quantitative restrictions	Currency board, with rate fixed to US$
Macedonia		
Average tariff of 4.7% in 1993. Quotas on only 4% of imports (mostly agriculture, imposed seasonally). Over 90% of imports free of licensing requirements	Over 90% of exports free of licensing requirements	Floating rate
Moldova		
New import tariff schedule adopted in November 1993 which reduces average tariff to about 30%. A few commodities at a maximum rate of 100%. Few licences, mainly for health, national security or environment reasons	5% surcharge on certain exports to the Former Soviet Union (FSU). Licensing requirements for 77 export categories. Export quotas on leather, energy products and cereals	Market-based floating rate. Barter trade disallowed with convertible currency countries
Poland		
Average weighted tariff 11% on industrial products and 18% on agricultural goods. Quotas on wheat, cars, alcohol, cigars, cigarettes, engine oil and petrol	Minimal export restrictions	Pre-announced crawling peg regime
Romania		
Average weighted tariff 11.7%, maximum rate 40%	Export quotas on raw materials for conservation reasons and drugs for price support reasons. Occasional export bans on food, fruits and wood products. Reduced export licensing requirements since June 1993	Floating exchange rate
Russia		
Relatively free of quotas and licensing requirements. Weighted average tariff raised to 14% in July 1994. Excise duties of 10-400% on some products	Wide range of tariff and non-tariff restrictions. Export of strategic goods, mainly raw materials, only by registered exporters. Introduction of commodity passports in 1994 to limit capital flight. Quotas on most energy and raw material products (two-thirds of total exports in 1993). Scope of quota and licensing systems reduced in early 1994, but scrapping postponed until 1995	New rouble zone planned with Belarus and Tadjikistan
Slovak Republic		
Quantitative import restrictions on some agricultural products, textiles, clothing, steel and coal	Export licensing for livestock and plants, some natural resources, and products such as textiles and steel which are subject to quotas in other countries	Peg to DM/US$
Slovenia		
Generally tariff-free. Where tariffs are applied, rates range up to a maximum of 25%. Customs formality tax of 1%. Some quotas on agricultural and textile products (98% of products are free of quotas)	Temporary export duties of 10-25% on raw materials. Permit for export of 'susceptible goods'	Floating exchange rate
Ukraine		
Foreign trade recentralised in late 1993, leaving most transactions (both within and outside CIS) subject to bilateral agreements and state order system. A few tariff rates of up to 10% since January 1993, with a limited number of goods (including textiles, cars) facing tariffs of up to 50%. No significant quotas	Foreign trade recentralised in late 1993, leaving most transactions (both within and outside the CIS) subject to bilateral agreements and state order system (explicit export quotas and licences for virtually all products since March 1994). Export duties within state orders have been largely eliminated	Interim currency with heavy restrictions on convertibility. Floating with intervention. Multiple exchange rates are to be gradually united. Much foreign trade is 'underground'

Source: Transition Report, EBRD 1994

PROPERTY

Land and property issues may be a factor of overriding importance in a location search, either because of the unique scale/nature of the site sought by the company concerned, or because of important time pressures. It should be remembered, however, that 'good' property does not necessarily make the best location for every kind of company.

In most location decisions, consideration should be given early on in the search process to general availability and cost factors, and to issues such as lease terms, which may affect get-out options. Companies assessing prospective locations need to evaluate the suitability of lease and purchase options, taking into account the reasons for their investment, the risk involved and the flexibility and resale/re-lease opportunities for individual properties. Another point to consider is the possibility of taking advantage of the attractive reliefs and allowances for property transactions which countries offer from time to time on a temporary or long-term basis. A further consideration often related to land and property issues is the need for permits relating both to physical construction/alteration and control of pollution.

The particular merits of individual buildings or plots of land should form part of a company's evaluation of a few shortlisted options. The key issues, examined in this chapter, are:
● Lease terms across Europe;
● The lease or purchase decision;
● Office and industrial property costs across Europe (and a review of the market);
● Planning and operating permits;
● Role and range of property services in the attraction of inward investment.

Lease terms across Europe
The key features of lease terms across Europe are illustrated in Exhibit 8.1. The main considerations in any lease agreement include:
● The period of lease;
● Rent review periods;
● Basis of rent review – indexed or open market;
● Tenant's right to renew lease;
● Ability and obligations on sub-leasing property;
● Responsibility for repairs, maintenance and insurance;
● Uses permitted within lease;
● Service charges and their review period;
● Liability for other local charges such as property taxation.

Because of the unique situation in Eastern Europe, a number of additional factors are important when considering that region – for example the ability of foreign nationals to purchase land and the form of ownership (see Exhibit 8.2).

Lease or purchase?
The decision whether to buy or lease a facility involves the evaluation of a range of quantitative and qualitative factors which affect profitability. The initial consideration, of course, is the availability of funds and access to them – if these do not exist, there is no real option to purchase. But assuming the company does have a choice, it needs to evaluate the financial costs involved in both purchase and rental. Due to the timescale of the location decision process, these should be calculated using net present values.

The lease/purchase decision also involves consideration of: the need for flexibility; tax incentives/allowances for purchase and subsequent modifications; liability for maintenance; compliance with new regulations in a lease agreement; market trends.

New or existing property?
The construction of new premises offers potential advantages: it can create a special identity, meet specific needs (both technological and space-related), provide a competitive edge, avoid wasted space – and unnecessary costs – and provide an opportunity to exploit economic incentives such as those offered by enterprise zones in France and the UK. The decision to opt for new or existing property can simultaneously involve a decision about whether to purchase or lease, and will often include an evaluation of the procurement method and means of financing.

Office and industrial property costs
The costs of renting or purchasing buildings vary as much between, and within, the regions of individual countries as they do between European nations. Property costs are driven not only by the type and degree of demand, but also by a host of supply factors such as vacancy rates, the availability of land, the economic base of the area (which determines the existing supply), the structure and capability of the local property industry, interest rates, the support of financial institutions and the level of investment opportunities elsewhere.

Exhibits 8.4 and 8.5 show the average industrial and office rents for 1994 across Europe. Industrial rents are based on a single storey 1,500-2,000 sq m steel portal frame and brick construction unit, which represents a typical bespoke new development. Office rents are based on first-class suites of 500-1,000 sq m in prime locations such as central business districts or new out-of-town business parks.

Planning and operating permits
The impact of planning and operating permits may be fundamental to investment decisions; at the very least they can have a significant effect on

Exhibit 8.1: Lease conditions and transaction costs in Europe, 1994

	Austria	Belgium	Czech Republic	Denmark	Finland	France	Germany	Greece	Hungary	Ireland
Period of lease	3-5 years	9 years; right to break every 3 years	3-5 years	5-10 years	5-10 years	9 years, right to break every 3 years	5-10 years, renewal option for further 5 years	6 years	1-3 years	5-35 years
Right to renew at end of term	No automatic right of renewal	No automatic right of renewal	No automatic right of renewal	Incorporated within lease		Usually option to renew	Usually option to renew for further 1, 2 or 5 years	Yes, additional 3 years		Yes
Rent review period	Annual inflation indexation	Indexed annually with a review every 3 years	No official provision for indexation	Annually by fixed percentage or indexed with an open-market review every 4 years	Annually	Annual or triennial indexation. Open-market rent reviews at end of lease	Reviewed periodically in line with open-market level or cost of living index	After 2 years, then annually	Provision for indexation common	Open-market review eve 5 years
VAT payable on rents	10% recoverable if lessee is a corporation	No	No	Payable on industrial property		VAT 18.6% (recoverable) or stamp duty at 2.5%	14% VAT	No		No
Service charge		12-25%	No		10% on offices	15-30%	10-15% on offices	No		5-10%
Additional costs	Internal repairs, insurance	Internal repairs, insurance, local taxes	Internal repairs	Insurance and internal repairs. Rent normally includes property tax	Internal repairs	Internal repairs, insurance and local taxes	Internal repairs and any increase in local taxes	Internal repairs, local taxes		Internal re insurance local taxes
Transaction costs: selling/freehold										
Legal		3%	0.75%	0.5%	Flat rate	1%	1.25%	3.25%		1%
Brokerage		3%	3-6%	2-3.5%	2-4%	5% neg.	3-5%	2%		1%
Transfer tax		12.5%	5%	1.2%	1.6%	18.2%	2%	23%		6%
Other costs		20.5% VAT on brokerage fees	5% VAT on purchase price	25% VAT on fees		18.6% VAT on brokerage and legal fees	14% VAT on all fees			21% VAT o all fees
Letting										
Legal	1 month's rent	0.5%	None	1%		1%				Hourly bas
Brokerage	3 months' rent	15% of first year's rent	3-6%	10-12%		30% of first year's rent (negotiable)		3.4%		10% of rer
Transfer tax	1%	12.5%	None	1%		No				1% of rent
Other costs		20.5% VAT on brokerage fees		25% VAT on fees		2.5% marginal local tax. 18.6% VAT on all fees	14% VAT on all fees			25% VAT on all fees

Source: ICPA 1994, Healy & Baker, 1994, Sinclair Roche & Temperley, 1994 Jones Lang Wootton, 1994

The construction of new premises can create a special identity, meet specific needs and provide a competitive edge

the time it takes to commence operations. Companies should therefore establish at an early stage whether these are likely to be an important or minor issue in the location evaluation. (The importance of such considerations will, of course, vary according to individual companies and projects. Service sector projects moving to established office zones will be less affected than, for example, a greenfield food-processing or pharmaceutical production facility.)

The focus of this chapter is to illustrate the importance and inter-relationship of development and pollution-related permits and consents. (For detailed information about the EU requirement for environmental impact assessments on all large-scale development proposals, see Chapter 13, 'The Environment'.)

The number and inter-relationships of permits vary greatly across Europe, as do the risks, costs, procedures and timescales involved in obtaining them. There may also be significant differences between local interpretation and implementation within individual countries and regions. The key types of permits that may be required are:
- Planning consent/development permit for construction or alteration of a building;
- Listed building consent (where there is special protection for historic buildings considered worthy of conservation);
- Building regulations;

Italy	Netherlands	Norway	Poland	Portugal	Spain	Sweden	Switzerland	UK
6 years	5-10 years	3-10 years	5 years	Standard annual term	5-10 years	3-10 years	5-10 years	5-20 years (tenant break options at 5 and 10 years)
Renewal option for continuous occupation	Renewal option for further 5 years	Renewal option for 3-5 years	No automatic right	Automatic right of renewal	No automatic right of renewal. By-agreement	Effective right at an open-market rent at end of lease	No automatic right	Set rules for landlord to refuse renewal
Annual increase of 75% of RPI. 2% registration tax on rent (landlord and tenant paying 1% each)	Indexed annually and there is an open-market review at end of the initial period	Indexed annually	Paid in US$ or DM	Indexed annually	Indexed annually to inflation	Indexed annually. Open-market review at end of lease	Annually indexed	Open-market rent review every 5 years
19%	17.5%	No	22%	No	16%	At 25%, may be changed by landlord	No	17.5%
10-15%	Dfl35-50 per sq.m	Included in rent	Included in rent	Included in rent	Paid by tenant		10-15%	10-15%
Internal repairs	Smaller internal repairs, insurance, a third of maintenance, property tax and variable proportion of local taxes	Internal repairs and maintenance	Internal repairs and maintenance. Rent includes property tax	Internal repairs. Rent includes property taxes and maintenance of common parts	Internal repairs, insurance and city taxes	Internal repairs and maintenance	Internal repairs	Structural and internal repairs, local taxes
0.5%	0.1-0.5%	Negotiable	5% (max $2,000)	1%	3.5%	0.1-1.0%	1%	0.5%
4%	2%	1.5-2.5% neg.	2.6-2.8%	3.75%	5%	1%	2-3%	1.5%
10%	1.2-6%	2.5%	N/A	10%	6%	3%	3%	1%
19% VAT on all fees	17.5% VAT on all fees	No VAT on fees	VAT	17% VAT on all fees	16% VAT	25% VAT on fees	6.5% on fees	17.5% VAT on all fees
0.5%	0.1-0.5%	Flat rate	1%	1% neg.	3.5%			0.5%
10%	10-16% for first year	Flat rate	50% of 1 month's rent	1 month's rent	4%		7%	10%
10%				0.5-10%	No	No		1%
19% VAT on all fees	17.5% VAT on all fees	No VAT on fees	VAT on fees	17% VAT on value of deed	No	25% VAT on fees	6.5% VAT on fees	17.5% VAT on all fees

- Fire certificate;
- Demolition consent;
- Water abstraction;
- Discharge of effluent;
- Air emissions;
- Waste disposal;
- Use and storage of hazardous substances;
- Noise permits;
- Consents relating to economic development.

There are many routine/minor developments that do not require permission or consent. However, any changes that will materially alter the physical nature of a building, its use or the type of material stored within it will, throughout Europe, require some form of approval. Typically, planning consent, fire certificates and building regulations are the dominant concerns for most companies. Their relationship with other consents in selected countries is illustrated in Exhibit 8.3.

Where there is a requirement for numerous consents, firms will have to deal with a number of different organisations. Whether these have a local, regional or national remit will affect their responsiveness and ability to co-ordinate their activities with other agencies.

The degree of integration of permits also differs throughout Europe. In France, for example, development consents, means of fire protection and construction are all covered by a single

The number of permits varies greatly across Europe, as do the risks, costs and timescales involved in obtaining them

Exhibit 8.2: Property law in Eastern Europe 1994

Issue	Poland	Hungary	Romania
Types of tenure and ownership by nationals	Resident nationals can own and lease both land and buildings	Resident nationals can own and lease both land and buildings	Resident nationals can own and lease both land and buildings. Agricultural land limited to 100 hectares
Ownership by foreign nationals	Foreign nationals can own and lease both land and buildings. Permit necessary for all but short-term tenancies, i.e. up to 10 and 30 years for offices and agricultural land respectively	Foreign nationals can own and lease both land and buildings (still subject to government permit) through Hungarian subsidiary	Foreign nationals cannot own or lease land or buildings; can only obtain user concessions. Can acquire leases of up to 49 years through local joint-venture companies or subsidiaries
Freedom of transfer	Land and leases other than short tenancies may be transferred subject to government permit for foreign nationals	Land, leases and buildings may be transferred and should be registered	Land may be transferred between resident nationals. Leases can be transferred to other resident nationals or to joint venture with locals
Restrictions on lease terms	Long-term lease (or perpetual usufruct) restricted to 99 years and only available from certain government agencies	No maximum period	It is difficult to secure leases beyond (to date) 49 years. Otherwise no restrictions
Mortgages	Possible to register mortgage on both freehold and long leases but register not conclusive, e.g. unsecured bank loans take priority	Mortgages can be created and must be registered in the Land Registry	Mortgages with limited enforcement rights can be created over land
Title	There is a formal registration system for both freeholds and leaseholds	There is a formal registration system; leaseholds are not registrable	There are limited areas with registration of title but still only conclusive evidence for commercial property is by ministerial certificates
Expropriation	Expropriation possible only in cases of necessity and subject to compensation	Possible if in the public interest. Subject to compensation	Expropriation possible only in cases of necessity and subject to compensation
Restitution	Restitution is possible but new proposals limit this, so will not affect purchasers (time limit of 6 months)	Time limits for restitution claims have not expired	No restitution rights except for agricultural land up to 10 hectares
Taxes	Corporation tax at 40%. Certain tax exemptions for non-residents. 5-6% stamp duty on transfer of ownership, 1% stamp duty on lease rentals	Corporate tax at 36%. VAT at 25%. 2-5% stamp duty and transfer tax of 2-8%	Corporation tax 45%. 30% for small companies. Tax holidays under foreign investment law. Stamp duty at 16%

Source: Sinclair Roche & Temperley 1994. NB: Position is for May 1994 but changes frequently

The availability of suitable properties at competitive prices is an important part of the location package

Exhibit 8.3: Development-related consents

	England and Wales	France	Germany	Netherlands	Spain
1 Construction					
1a Development	● Planning permission	● Building permit and sub-division controls	● Building permit	● Building permit	● Building permit ● First occupation licence
1b Alteration of building of historic or architectural importance	● Listed building consent		● Building permit	● Building permit	● Building permit ● First occupation licence
2 Building form and structure					
	● Building regulations approval ● Demolition notice ● Fire certificate	● Permis de démolir	● Building permit	● Building permit	● Building permit ● First occupation licence
3 Pollution control					
3a Emission/discharges	● Discharge consent ● IPC authorisation	● Authorisation	● Authorisation ● Discharge authorisation	● Discharge licence ● Environmental permit	● Emissions authorisation ● Discharge authorisation
3b Hazardous substances	● Hazardous substances consent	● Hazardous substances authorisation.			● Hazardous substances authorisation
3c Waste disposal	● Waste-disposal licence	● Waste authorisation.	● Waste-disposal authorisation		● Waste authorisation
4 Regional economic development					
		● Consent for relocation of tertiary employment			
5 Water abstraction					
			● Water abstraction licence		
Summary: number of consents					
a required for all projects	2	1	1	1	2
b possibly also required	8	7	4	3	5

Source: HMSO, 1993. Consents in bold type are required for all projects (except those below certain size thresholds); the others might also be required, depending on the nature of the development.

Czech Republic	Slovakia	Bulgaria
Resident nationals can own and lease both land and buildings	Resident nationals can own and lease both land and buildings	Resident nationals can own and lease both land and buildings. Limits on ownership of agricultural land have been lifted
Non-residents cannot own but can lease land or buildings. Subject to certain exceptions, may own through a Czech subsidiary	Non-residents cannot own but can lease land or buildings. Subject to certain exceptions, may own through a Slovak subsidiary	Foreign nationals cannot generally own or lease land except through a wholly owned Bulgarian company, but may own buildings and, in certain areas, non-agricultural land. May do so through Bulgarian subsidiary (except agricultural land)
Land, leases and buildings may be transferred subject to their terms	Land, leases and buildings may be transferred subject to their terms	Land, leases and buildings may be transferred subject to restrictions, e.g. land allocated from the municipal land stock cannot be resold within 10 years
There are restrictions on the freedom to negotiate rent, duration and certain other lease terms	There are restrictions on the freedom to negotiate rent, duration and certain other lease terms	The general restriction on leases to 10 years has been abolished
Mortgages possible but not adequately regulated. Enforcement procedures not fully developed	Mortgages possible but not adequately regulated. Enforcement procedures not fully developed	Mortgages exist but foreigners have difficulties in taking security
There is a system of centralised land registers. Not yet complete and cannot be fully relied on	There is a system of centralised land registers. Not yet complete and cannot be fully relied on	Privately owned title is generally registered either with the municipal land commission or notary public
Expropriation possible only in cases of necessity and subject to compensation	Expropriation possible only in cases of necessity and subject to compensation	Expropriation possible only in cases of necessity and subject to compensation
Restitution claims had to be lodged by December 1992	Restitution claims had to be lodged by December 1992	Restitution available but only for claims lodged prior to June 1993
Corporation tax at 45%. Income tax from 15-47%. VAT rate 23%. Transfer taxes at 1-20%	Corporation tax at 45%. Income tax from 15-47%. VAT rate 23%. Transfer taxes are also payable up to 20%	Corporation tax at 40%. 30% for small companies and those with foreign investment over 49%. Transfer taxes. VAT at 11%

Inability to provide property solutions within an investing company's timescale will rule out many locations at an early stage

building permit, whereas in the UK three individual consents are required. Integration does not necessarily mean straightforward approval, as the various elements may still be dealt with by different departments and need to be approved sequentially, therefore increasing the time needed to obtain a particular consent.

Companies investing in a location may also face restrictions regarding who can make a development application. This is the case in Germany, where only the land owner or a qualified architect can apply for building consent. In countries such as the UK there is no such requirement.

Property as an inward investment tool

Property is just one of many location requirements and thus should constitute only part of a comprehensive range of services/tools/benefits promoted by the inward investment/economic development agencies. However, the availability of suitable properties at competitive prices is an important part of the comprehensive location package, as it gives investing companies a yardstick with which to compare competing areas. Inability to provide property solutions within an investing company's timescale will, moreover, rule out many locations at an early stage.

Development agencies that do not or cannot provide investors with property directly can find themselves at a disadvantage, especially if competing agencies are in a position to negotiate property deals for investors. They can, however, facilitate the provision and effective marketing of property. Many of them will, for instance, work closely with organisations involved in the strategic assessment and provision of land.

Agencies need an up-to-date, comprehensive database of available existing property and land, and also need to be aware of pipeline developments. They should seek to provide a comprehensive property service which should include: familiarising companies with the nature of the property sector and any laws relating to it; providing information packs on properties and their locality; arranging tours of properties conducted by well-briefed representatives; handling design-and-build and property financing requirements.

With an appropriate allocation of a range of sites and a comprehensive property service as outlined above, those agencies that cannot themselves provide property for investors are in a better position to compete with rival organisations in other regions, even those that negotiate property deals directly.

Exhibit 8.3: Average office rents

- Very low cost
- Low cost
- Average cost
- High cost
- Very high cost

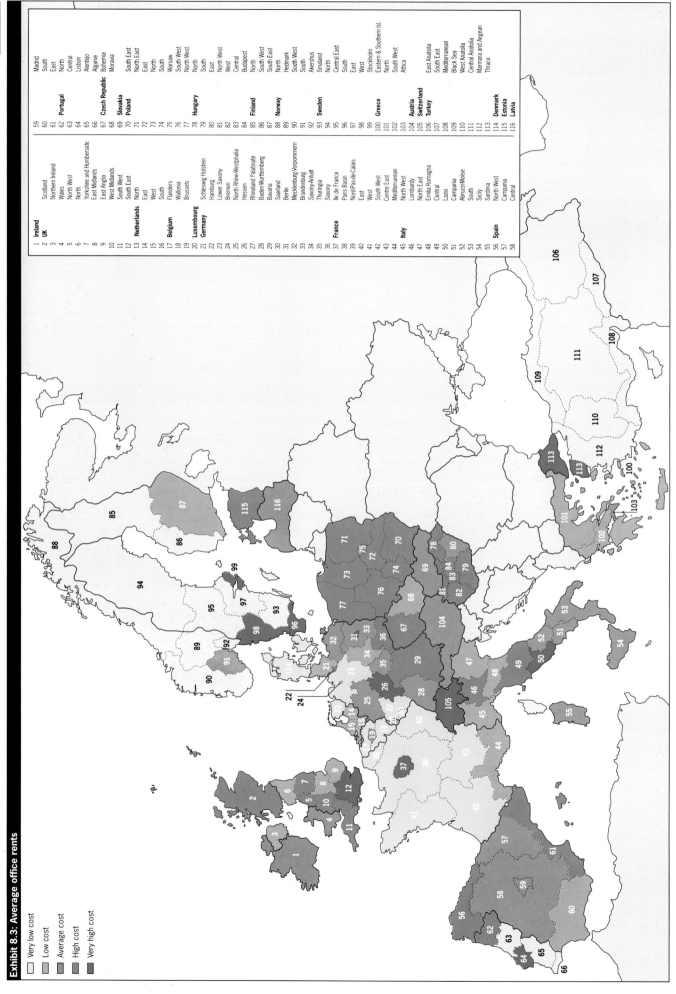

Ireland
1 Ireland

UK
2 Scotland
3 Northern Ireland
4 Wales
5 North West
6 North
7 Yorkshire and Humberside
8 East Midlands
9 East Anglia
10 West Midlands
11 South West
12 South East

Netherlands
13 North
14 East
15 West
16 South

Belgium
17 Flanders
18 Wallonia
19 Brussels

Luxembourg
20

Germany
21 Schleswig Holstein
22 Hamburg
23 Lower Saxony
24 Bremen
25 North Rhine-Westphalia
26 Hessen
27 Rhineland Palatinate
28 Baden-Württemberg
29 Bavaria
30 Saarland
31 Berlin
32 Mecklenburg-Vorpommern
33 Brandenburg
34 Saxony-Anhalt
35 Thuringia
36 Saxony

France
37 Ile de France
38 Paris Basin
39 Nord-Pas-de-Calais
40 East
41 West
42 South West
43 Centre East
44 Mediterranean
45 North West

Italy
46 Lombardy
47 North East
48 Emilia Romagna
49 Central
50 Lazio
51 Campania
52 Abruzzi/Molise
53 South
54 Sicily
55 Sardinia

Spain
56 North West
57 Campania
58 Central

59 Madrid
60 South
61 East
62 North
63 Central
Portugal
64 Lisbon
65 Alentejo
66 Algarve
Czech Republic
67 Bohemia
68 Moravia
Slovakia
69
Poland
70 South East
71 North East
72 East
73 North
74 South
75 Warsaw
76 South West
77 North West
Hungary
78 North
79 South
80 East
81 North West
82 West
83 Central
84 Budapest
Finland
85 North
86 South West
87 South East
Norway
88 North
89 Hedmark
90 South West
91 South
92 Akershus
93 Smaland
Sweden
94 North
95 Central East
96 South
97 East
98 West
99 Stockholm
Greece
100 Eastern & Southern Isl.
101 North
102 South West
103 Attica
Austria
104
Switzerland
105
Turkey
106 East Anatolia
107 South East
108 Mediterranean
109 Black Sea
110 West Anatolia
111 Central Anatolia
112 Marmara and Aegean
113 Thrace
Denmark
114
Estonia
115
Latvia
116

60

Exhibit 8.4: Average industry rents

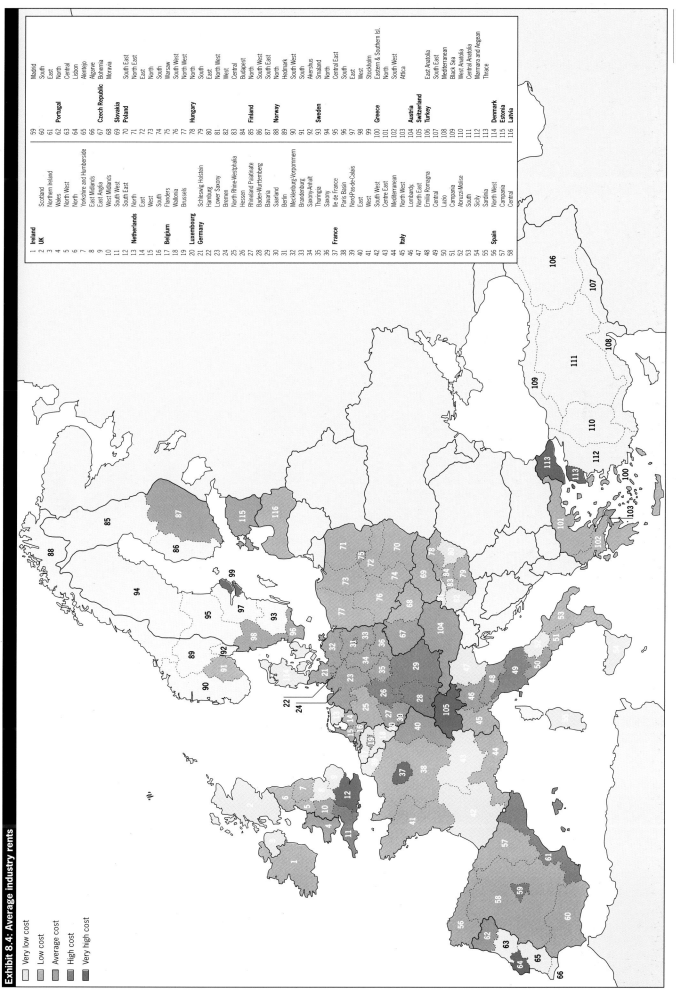

Chapter 9

TELECOMMUNICATIONS

The cost, quality and scope of telecommunication services are of increasing importance to companies' location decisions. Spending on telecoms can represent as much as 8 per cent of total expenditure for banking and financial service firms, with computer service companies spending even more. It is a key factor too for international headquarters and data-processsing centres, and also for the increasing number of pan-European call centres. These include:

● Customer help-line services such as those provided for computer software users;
● Reservation centres for hotel chains and airlines;
● Direct sales operations;
● Telephone mail-order services.

Improved telecommunication links open up new opportunities for Europe's regions. Regions that have invested heavily in improving their telecommunication networks can, for example, provide additional value-added services with which to attract international mobile businesses (this is especially true in the growing multimedia sector). A number of telecommunications companies, such as the recently privatised Dutch KPN, are active in promoting inward investment into their country.

But improving telecommunications bring new threats as well as new opportunities: tasks such as data processing and keyboard entry can now be undertaken in low-wage developing countries, with the result that we are witnessing a transfer of clerical work from Europe to Asia.

Telecommunications in Europe: an overview

The telecommunications industry today is undergoing unparalleled technological and regulatory change. As a result, users will benefit greatly from:

● The development of new services which will allow faster, more efficient communication;
● Increased competition and a resulting emphasis on competitive pricing and quality of service.

Although public carriers still dominate in basic domestic sectors, competition is increasing in data services and mobile communications. In anticipation of even greater competition in the near future, public telecommunications investment is increasing, and state monopolies are instituting new management practices to improve their overall competitive position both within the Western European market and in Eastern Europe and the CIS. This chapter examines:

● State monopolies and the liberalisation of the European telecommunications market;
● Infrastructure development, and new technologies currently available to users;

● Competitive pricing, and the comparative quality of service levels between telecoms providers;
● The developing Eastern European and CIS telecommunications market.

State monopolies and liberalisation

Historically, telecommunications services in Europe have been provided by state monopolies developed with the support of national governments. These monopolies have been protected from competition by the high investment costs of installing land-lines: necessary to connect individual users to the nearest exchange, land-lines are comprised in part of copper loops, either buried underground or raised on telegraph poles. The enormous costs associated with the installation of these loops have traditionally been insurmountable barriers to entry. However, the provision of microwave and satellite technology has made some wiring redundant, and mobile telecommunications outside the scope of the copper loop are now possible.

Liberalisation of the data services and mobile communications markets in many European countries has allowed for increased competition, and state providers now find themselves challenged by national and multinational carriers and computer companies with sophisticated products and aggressive marketing/promotion techniques.

Within Europe, the UK has aggressively liberalised and privatised its domestic telecommunications industry. The privatisation of British Telecom occurred at the same time that Mercury Communications, a division of Cable and Wireless, came into being. By creating two competing telecom providers, the British government sought to encourage the development of genuine competition and discourage the creation of merely a privatised monopoly. Mercury was allowed access to certain lines and facilities, and the company originally prospered by aggressively targeting both business and long-distance markets. It has also entered the mobile market. More recently, the UK market has become even more competitive, as cable television companies and new players such as AT&T have also begun to provide telecommunication services.

Competition within countries for basic domestic telephone services is still very rare, however. The UK remains the only country in Europe where there is competition in the basic provision of voice telephone services. It was also the first country to separate the provision of telephone services from regulation, though most EU members have now separated out their regulatory function. Austria, Sweden, Switzerland, Italy and Turkey continue to possess a single regulatory and statutory body.

Improving telecoms bring new threats as well as new opportunities: tasks such as data processing can now be undertaken in low-wage countries

The UK remains the only country in Europe where there is competition in the basic provision of voice telephone services

There are several specific areas of the telecommunications industry that tend to be liberalised first, including the equipment market and the Value Added Network Services (VANS) market.

Most European countries now allow equipment to be sold competitively by more than one supplier, although in a number of countries some restrictions still apply. In Luxembourg, for example, the government must supply the first handset to users.

Liberalisation has allowed for increased competition between the large international VANS providers. VANS allow for additional advancements to basic services, usually related to computers. VANS can, for example, allow for the re-routing of calls when engaged, or the routing of long-distance calls in the least expensive manner. Increased handset capacity through digitisation and micro-technology will, along with the development of a broadband infrastructure, continue to increase the importance of VANS systems.

In Eastern European countries, moves towards a more open market are likely to be held back by older technology. Existing infrastructures that have not been developed to conform to international standards are unlikely to interface with the more modern, complex European and American systems already in place worldwide. As new equipment is installed in these countries over time, their systems should become more compatible. Initially, however, the market for new providers of equipment will be limited.

The European Commission has set a specific deadline – 1 January 1998 – for the full liberalisation of public voice telephone services throughout the EU. From that date, any provider of telecommunications services and/or equipment will be free to compete throughout Europe provided they have obtained a licence to operate.

At the same time, the Commission has recognised that two-level competition is inevitable, at least in the short term. Belgium, France, Germany, Italy, the Netherlands and the UK are expected to be able to compete on an equal basis straight away, while Ireland, Portugal and Spain will probably need at least five years to provide comparable services.

The opening up of services has seen increasing pressure to privatise state-owned telecommunication companies in a number of countries: Telecom Italia, KPN in the Netherlands (which still retains its postal services, unlike other privatised telecom companies) and Tele Denmark have all recently made their first appearance on the stock markets.

The telecommunications infrastructure
Basic voice and data transmission systems are in place in all European countries, though the number of available main lines can vary considerably. Exhibit 9.1 (above right) ranks different countries by GDP per capita and population for each main telephone line.

In 1990, overall capital investment in Europe was the equivalent of Ecu120 per person. This level of investment was reached despite fears that the trend towards deregulation and competition would divert funds from public infrastructure towards private networks. In fact, the move away from monopoly provision of telecommunication services has resulted in a clear increase

in overall infrastructure investment. Levels of investment do, however, vary from country to country, and from region to region (see Exhibit 9.2, below).

Investment can be broken down into two main categories:
● Investment for the expansion of large existing systems (as in Germany and Switzerland);
● Investment for modernisation of smaller systems (as in Italy and Spain).

Although overall investment is a difficult indicator to interpret, it is possible to estimate what percentage has been due to network expansion, and what percentage has been due to modernisation. European countries have devoted roughly a fifth of their investment expenditure to expansion, with the rest going towards modernisation (most notably the change from analogue to digital systems, see below) and the introduction of new services.

Digitisation
The increases in public sector telecommunications investment that we have been witnessing over the past ten years have been due in part to

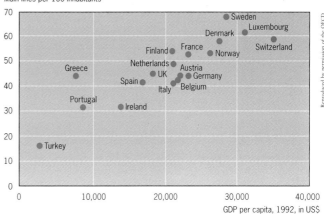
Exhibit 9.1: Telephone main lines per 100 inhabitants and GDP per capita
Source: OECD *Communications Outlook* 1995

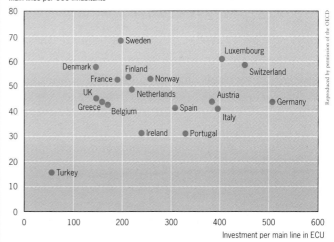
Exhibit 9.2: Investment per line and main lines per 100 inhabitants
Source: OECD *Communications Outlook* 1995

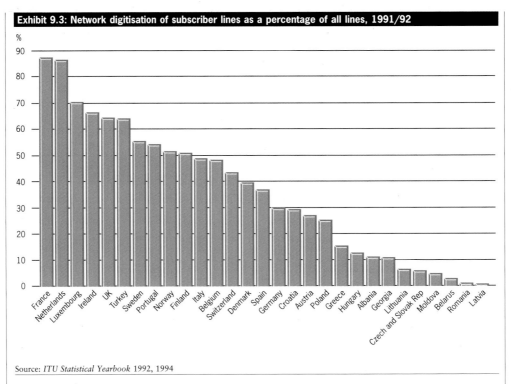

Exhibit 9.3: Network digitisation of subscriber lines as a percentage of all lines, 1991/92

Source: *ITU Statistical Yearbook* 1992, 1994

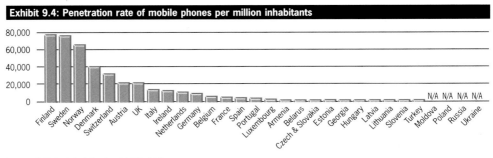

Exhibit 9.4: Penetration rate of mobile phones per million inhabitants

Source: *ITU Statistical Yearbook* 1992, 1994

the significant investment necessary to switch from analogue to digital technology. Digital technology allows for:
● Higher quality service;
● Lower maintenance costs;
● A lower unit cost per line in the long term;
● Lower operating costs, due to more compact switching equipment and less manual intervention by operators.

Importantly, in countries where there is increased competition, public telecoms have been forced by regulation to digitise in order to make interconnection to new networks possible. (Exhibit 9.3, above, shows the network digitisation of subscriber lines.)

One of the most important benefits of digitisation derives from the technology involved, which allows for several different types of service over the same network. These services include:
● Voice communication;
● Transfer of text and data;
● Transfer of images (unavailable in most European countries at this time).

Digital technology will eventually force total deregulation of the industry, as it will be impossible for regulators to draw boundaries between protected services and unprotected ones. Digitisation will therefore encourage open com-

petition both between existing public telecoms providers and new, private firms.

Mobile communications
Because the technology is new and the costs of ownership are particularly high, mobile communication services have only become widely available in the past 10 years. However, the introduction of digital technology should improve mobile transmission quality and allow for lower overall operating and running costs. In the decade to come, prospects are good for the widespread utilisation of mobile communications by a wide variety of users.

The cost of mobile communications
In Europe, different countries are at varying stages in the development and use of mobile communications. Exhibit 9.4 details the number of mobile phones in use in a selected group of countries for which information is available. Although penetration levels are fast increasing in most countries, the ranking is likely to remain roughly as shown.

Tariffs in various countries have significantly impacted on the general use of mobile communications. In most Nordic countries and also in Switzerland, for example, lower tariffs have encouraged high usage (Exhibit 9.5 gives a comparison of tariffs in different countries). This reflects a conscious decision in those countries –

Digital technology will eventually force total deregulation of the industry

Digitisation will encourage open competition both between existing public telecoms providers and new, private firms

Exhibit 9.5: OECD basket of mobile communications charges, January 1994

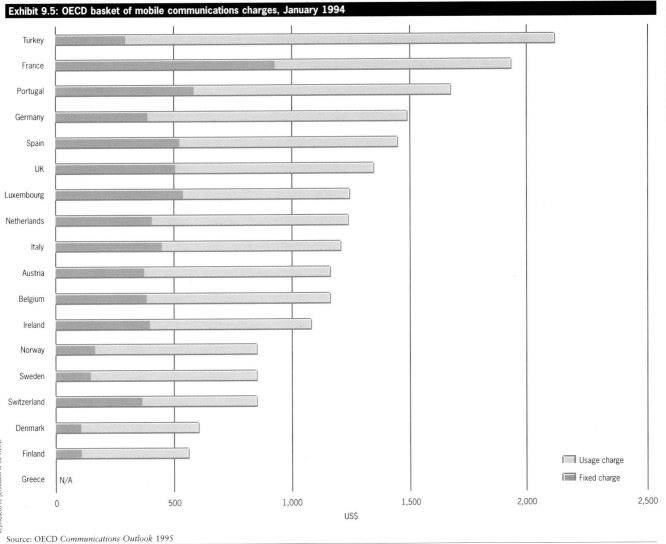

Legend: Usage charge / Fixed charge

US$

Source: OECD *Communications Outlook* 1995

prompted by the high cost of installing and maintaining land links – to promote demand, resulting in the highest penetration figures in Europe. In most other European countries, the domain of cellular services has been restricted to a single operator. However, two-thirds of countries have announced their intention to license at least one competitive mobile communications operator, and this will certainly allow for greater overall competition.

Pricing

Price comparisons have been limited largely to Western Europe, the US and Japan. Using calls to the US and Japan as standards, where data is available it is possible to compare prices. Exhibit 9.6 ranks the cost of a one-minute call from different European countries to the US and Japan.

The transfer of data may be particularly important to multinational companies, and prices for this service tend to differ dramatically from

Exhibit 9.6: Cost of a one-minute call to the US and Japan

Country	Call to US (US$)	Call to Japan (US$)
UK (BT)	0.64	1.65
UK (Mercury)	0.65	1.66
Norway	0.71	1.06
Sweden	0.89	1.77
France	1.00	1.92
Ireland	1.01	1.76
Belgium	1.02	1.45
Switzerland	1.02	1.62
Netherlands	1.05	1.88
Italy	1.16	1.76
Germany	1.19	1.89
Denmark	1.23	1.97
Luxembourg	1.26	2.36
Portugal	1.30	1.91
Greece	1.31	2.04
Spain	1.53	3.07

Source: Tariffica, Sept 1994

Exhibit 9.7: Cost per hour for connection, rental and use of packet-switched data networks

Country	Cost US$
UK	nil
Portugal	4.86
Finland	5.12
Germany	5.44
Spain	5.66
Denmark	6.02
Switzerland	6.09
Netherlands	6.22
Norway	6.24
France	6.36
Sweden	6.55
Belgium/Luxembourg	6.94
Italy	7.56
Austria	10.32
Ireland	11.42
Greece	13.69

Source: Tariffica, Sept 1994

New technology and an emphasis on quality have led to shorter waiting times for new lines and reductions in the frequency of call failures

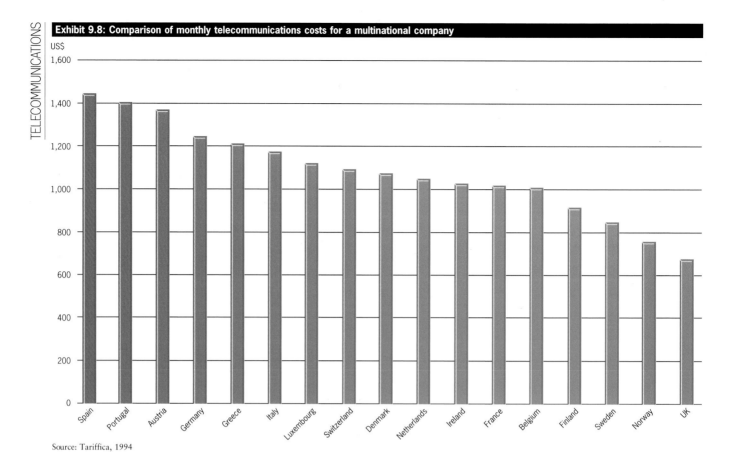

Exhibit 9.8: Comparison of monthly telecommunications costs for a multinational company

US$

Source: Tariffica, 1994

Exhibit 9.9: Quality of service

	Call failure rates in 1992 (%)				Faults	Waiting time
	Local calls	Trunk calls	Overall	Fault incidence per 100 lines	Repair time % cleared in 24 hrs per year	for a new connection (days*)
Austria	0.8	1.6		18.8	93.0	45
Belgium	2.2			9.4	58.0	15
Denmark			1.9	n/a	95.1	0
Finland	3.2	0.8		10.8	68.7	5
France	0.6			8.2	93.0	15**
Germany	n/a			11.6	n/a	n/a
Greece	n/a			53.7	58.6	789
Ireland	1.3	1.8		38.0	85.0	19
Italy	4.0	5.8		12.8	94.4	15
Luxembourg		4.0		16.7	75.0	n/a
Netherlands	n/a			5.1	100.0	n/a
Norway	1.4	2.4		16.0	89.0	7
Portugal			4.0	52.0	79.0	120
Spain	0.4	1.5		43.2	80.0	45
Sweden	0.7	0.9		9.5	94.0	0
Switzerland	0.4	0.4		40.0	86.8	3
Turkey	0.5	0.1		64.0	95.0	150
UK	0.2	0.2		17.0	81.7	8***

*Where waiting time is listed as 0, service connection is usually available at the end of the following day. ** France Telecom met 91.6% of orders within 15 days *** BT met 86.5% of orders within 8 days Source: OECD *Communications Outlook* 1995

country to country. Exhibit 9.7 ranks the rate per hour for connection, rental and use of packet-switched data networks in different European countries. (BT and Mercury in the UK do not charge any duration costs to international destinations for data.) Exhibit 9.8 provides a comparison of monthly costs for a multinational company based in a capital city.

Quality of service

Comparable quality-of-service indicators are notoriously difficult to obtain. However, it is generally the case that new technology and an emphasis on improved quality have led to shorter waiting times for new lines as well as reductions in the frequency of call failures and line faults.

Exhibit 9.9 shows improvements in quality of service in various European countries. (It should be noted that the definitions of individual indicators generally follow the measures used in each individual country and may therefore not be wholly comparable.)

Telecommunications in Eastern Europe

The telecommunications technology currently in use in Eastern Europe is generally some 30 years older than the Western equivalent.

Exhibit 9.10: Cellular telephone subscribers 1993 (per 10,000 people)

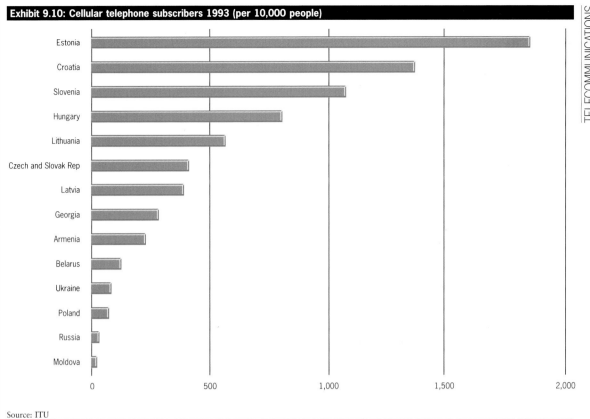

Source: ITU

Exhibit 9.11: New telephone lines, percentage change 1989-92

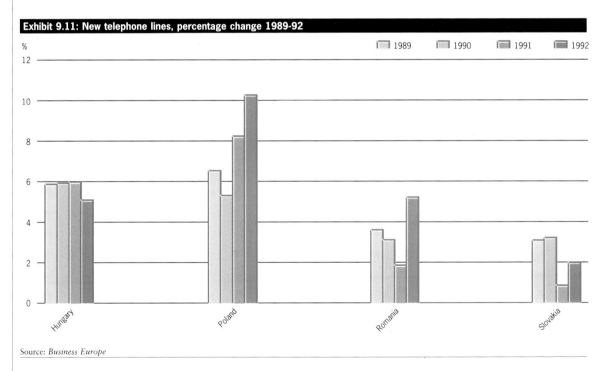

Source: *Business Europe*

Problems and opportunties

Electromechanical rather than electronic – let alone digital – exchanges are the norm in the region, and in rural areas exchanges are often still manual. Obviously, this situation represents a potential burden for inward investors – but it is also a superb market opportunity for suppliers and operators of equipment.

In Hungary, for example, research carried out in 1992 revealed that the country's switching-equipment dated from the 1920s, and that some 10 per cent of its loop was paper-insulated. For users, the result was frequent breakdowns and cellular overloading. In Germany, meanwhile, it has been estimated that around DM55 billion (US$5 billion) is required to bring the old East German telecommunications system up to Western standards. Although funds for this kind of investment are not available in other countries, the provision of new telephone lines is increasing rapidly.

Waiting lists for telephone lines in Eastern Europe remain extensive, however. In Poland, for example, the current waiting time is nine years. It is interesting to note that mobile telephone use is also taking off rapidly in Eastern Europe, although the level of use varies considerably, as does associated investment.

67

Chapter 10

ENERGY AND WATER

For major energy users – and particularly for energy-intensive processes such as glass, chemicals, paper and cement production – energy is a key factor to be taken into consideration when assessing potential locations: variations in energy costs between sites can have a major impact on a company's final profits.

Two important issues affecting the energy and water sectors are liberalisation and the environment. The former has involved the privatisation of state-owned monopolies, the opening up of competition and reductions in some energy prices. The latter has resulted in governments trying to reduce energy consumption, the development of alternative fuels, and pressure to raise the price of energy. Another important factor is, of course, security of supply. As Exhibit 10.2 illustrates, few European countries can meet their energy needs from indigenous production; heavy reliance on imports therefore influences many countries' energy policies.

The market share of each particular fuel varies considerably from country to country, reflecting indigenous sources of fuel. For example, Russia's vast supplies of natural gas mean that it can meet nearly half its energy requirements with gas, while Norway's topography allows it to use hydro-electricity for 46 per cent of its energy requirement. Meanwhile the lack of significant indigenous resources has encouraged both France and Sweden to make considerable use of nuclear energy.

The use of coal in Europe has declined dramatically due to environmental concerns and the increasing willingness of governments to sanction the use of gas to generate electricity. Ironically, reserves/production ratios – that is, the number of years it will take to exhaust known reserves at present production levels – show that while oil and gas reserves in Europe are relatively low, those for coal are considerable (see Exhibit 10.3).

Exhibit 10.1: Primary energy consumption, per capita and by type (1993)

	Oil %	Natural gas %	Coal %	Nuclear energy %	Hydro-electric %	Per capita (TOE*)
US	39.5	26.2	24.8	8.2	1.3	7.8
Switzerland	54.4	8.0	0.9	24.3	12.4	6.9
Estonia	30.0	11.7	58.2	–	–	6.1
Belgium/Luxembourg	48.1	17.4	15.5	18.8	–	5.4
Netherlands	46.0	42.7	10.2	1.1	–	5.2
Russia	24.7	49.5	19.5	4.2	2.1	4.9
Sweden	39.9	1.7	5.2	37.6	15.6	4.6
Finland	45.6	12.0	14.7	22.1	5.5	4.3
Norway	50.3	–	2.7	–	46.4	4.3
Czech Republic	17.2	12.2	63.3	7.5	0.3	4.2
Belarus	65.1	28.9	1.9	–	–	4.1
France	39.4	12.5	6.0	40.0	2.1	4.1
Germany	41.0	17.8	28.9	11.8	0.5	4.1
Slovakia	21.1	26.8	31.4	16.1	0.8	3.8
Japan	55.4	11.1	17.4	14.2	1.9	3.7
UK	39.1	28.1	23.6	9.0	0.2	3.7
Ukraine	15.9	44.0	29.6	10.2	0.4	3.7
Denmark	50.3	11.6	38.1	–	–	3.6
Lithuania	40.3	24.8	4.9	33.6	0.3	3.0
Austria	50.0	25.0	11.2	–	13.3	2.8
Italy	61.1	28.4	7.9	–	2.5	2.6
Poland	14.5	8.5	76.8	–	0.1	2.5
Greece	64.8	0.4	33.6	–	1.2	2.4
Hungary	33.7	34.2	16.9	14.8	–	2.4
Spain	55.9	6.3	18.7	15.8	2.3	2.4
Bulgaria	27.0	19.5	37.0	14.3	1.2	2.3
Ireland	58.3	17.9	23.8	–	1.2	2.3
Latvia	46.5	31.0	5.2	–	3.9	2.1
Moldova	39.8	39.4	21.7	–	0.4	1.9
Romania	27.6	44.3	24.8	–	2.4	1.9
Portugal	75.8	–	19.7	–	5.1	1.6
Turkey	46.1	7.7	41.5	–	4.9	1.0

* TOE = types of oil equivalent. Figures have been rounded so may not add up to 100. Source: Ernst & Young/*BP Statistical Review of World Energy 1994*/*Electricity in European Economies in Transition* OECD 1994

Energy is a key factor to be taken into consideration when assessing potential locations... Variations in energy costs can have a major impact on final profits

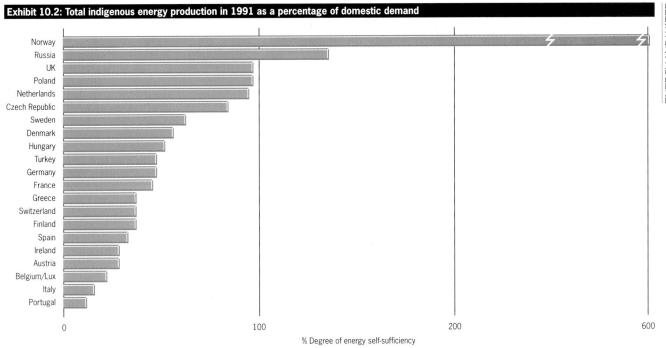

Exhibit 10.2: Total indigenous energy production in 1991 as a percentage of domestic demand

% Degree of energy self-sufficiency

Source: *World Competitiveness Report* 1994

Exhibit 10.3: Reserve/production ratios (years)

	Oil	Gas	Coal
Total OECD Europe	9.1	25.8	192
Total non-OECD Europe	19.9	68.9	329
Total world	43	65	236

Source: *BP Statistical Review of World Energy* 1994

Exhibit 10.4: Electricity imports and exports 1993 (TWh)

	Imports	Exports	Imports as % of total consumption
Austria	8.1	8.8	17.0
Belgium	7.6	5.4	10.4
Denmark	6.3	4.9	17.8
Finland	8.0	0.4	11.7
France	3.6	65.2	0.9
Germany	33.1	32.7	0.3
Greece	1.0	0.2	2.6
Italy	40.1	0.7	15.3
Luxembourg	4.5	0.4	84.9
Netherlands	10.8	0.1	12.3
Norway	0.8	8.6	0.7
Portugal	2.1	1.9	6.7
Spain	4.6	3.3	2.9
Sweden	8.0	8.6	5.5
Switzerland	19.5	26.7	36.2
Turkey	0.2	0.6	0.3
UK	16.7	0.1	4.9

Source: IEA/OECD energy statistics, 1994

Electricity

The price at which electricity is supplied to the final user is influenced both by the methods used to produce it, and the question of whether or not countries are dependent on imports to meet their energy requirements. Thus while countries such as Italy are heavily dependent on imported electricity, France has excess generating capacity and is a major exporter (see Exhibit 10.4, above).

Alternative generating methods – such as wind and solar power or the use of waste and biomass – are rapidly increasing, but from very low levels. It is estimated that they presently account for just 0.1 per cent of electricity output for the whole of Europe, a figure that is expected to rise to 0.7 per cent by the year 2010. As we see greater liberalisation and competition in the European energy sector, and as companies use the fuel of their choice to generate electricity, prices are likely to fall. As well as lower prices, competition from these alternative fuels is expected to bring greater efficiency gains. We are also witnessing a gradual shift away from coal to the use of natural gas in electricity generation.

Many Eastern European countries face major increases in electricity costs due to the need to close unsafe and/or life-expired nuclear plants. There are also environmental pressures to reduce the level of coal burnt, and considerable sums are being spent cleaning up emissions. The increased use of gas for electricity generation has raised concerns about over-dependency on Russia for supplies. This is one reason for France's strong support for the nuclear industry.

An increasing number of countries are moving away from a national tariff standard. It is therefore becoming increasingly difficult to compare costs between countries; it is clear, however, that electricity prices in most European countries are considerably higher than those in the US.

Gas

Most European countries are heavily dependent on imports to meet their demand for gas. The major sources of supply at present are Russia, the Netherlands, Norway and Algeria. To avoid over-dependency on any one source of supply, a number of countries are currently investigating the possibility of building a pipeline linking Europe with Iran, and further pipelines to the North African gas fields.

Natural gas supplies are not readily available in many parts of Europe, including Greece, Norway, Portugal, large areas of Spain, Finland, Sweden, Switzerland and Turkey. This is due to a lack of indigenous supplies and/or the country's topography, which makes the creation of a gas transmission network prohibitively expensive. However, a number of the above countries are

Many Eastern European countries face major increases in electricity costs due to the need to close unsafe nuclear plants

Exhibit 10.5: Methods of electricity production, 1992 (percentage of total electricity generated)

	Hydro–electric %	Geothermal %	Nuclear %	Natural gas %	Coal/oil/other %
Austria	71.3	–	–	13.5	15.2
Belarus	–	–	–	39.2	60.8
Belgium	1.7	–	60.2	9.3	28.8
Bulgaria	8.1	–	32.3	13.9	45.7
Czech Republic	2.6	–	20.2	2.2	75.0
Denmark	3.2	–	–	2.5	94.3
Estonia	–	–	–	11.6	88.4
Finland	27.4	–	33.3	8.9	30.4
France	16.2	–	72.9	0.7	10.2
Germany	4.2	–	30.2	6.2	59.5
Greece	6.9	–	–	0.2	92.9
Hungary	0.6	–	44.7	25.0	29.7
Ireland	6.9	–	–	23.1	70.0
Italy	21.1	1.5	–	15.8	61.6
Latvia	65.8	–	–	15.9	18.3
Lithuania	2.7	–	78.1	10.7	8.5
Luxembourg	52.2	–	–	4.5	43.3
Moldova	2.7	–	–	44.1	53.2
Netherlands	0.4	–	4.8	56.2	38.6
Norway	99.6	–	–	–	0.4
Poland	2.7	–	–	0.4	96.8
Portugal	17.4	–	–	–	82.6
Romania	21.6	–	–	36.5	41.9
Russia	17.1	–	11.9	41.3	29.7
Slovakia	8.9	–	53.3	10.0	27.8
Spain	13.7	–	35.4	1.1	49.8
Sweden	51.7	–	42.9	0.5	4.9
Switzerland	57.7	–	39.6	0.6	2.1
Turkey	39.4	0.1	–	16.1	44.4
UK	2.3	–	23.1	2.7	71.9
Ukraine	3.2	–	29.1	34.0	33.7

Source: IEA/OECD energy statistics, 1994

Reproduced by permission of the OECD

The fact that most countries in Eastern Europe are heavily reliant on imports of Russian gas is a cause of some concern

Exhibit 10.6: The state of Eastern European generating capacity

	Closure of unsafe power stations including nuclear	Refitting and modernisation of thermal units	Construction of new, clean thermal capacity	Development of renewable energy – hydro, geothermal, etc	Modernisation of retained nuclear units	Expansion and/or introduction of nuclear electricity programmes
Bulgaria	√			√	√	√
Czech Republic	√	√	√		√	√
Hungary				√	√	√
Poland	√	√	√			√
Romania					√	√
Slovakia	√	√	√		√	√

Source: Jeremy Russell in association with the Energy and Environmental Programme, the Royal Institute of International Affairs and the World Conservation Union

Exhibit 10.7: Electricity prices for industry, 1993 (US = 100)

Portugal	249.4
Switzerland	195.8
Turkey	194.7
Italy	189.8
Germany	182.7
Spain	173.8
Austria	146.7
Denmark	144.7
Luxembourg	141.8
UK	138.2
Belgium	122.1
Greece	121.8
Ireland	121.7
France	112.1
Netherlands	108.9
Hungary	108.2
Slovak Republic	102.2
Finland	99.3
Sweden	72.5
Norway	71.4
Poland	70.4
Russia	37.9

Source: IEA/OECD energy statistics, 1994

Exhibit 10.8: Natural gas prices for industry, 1993 (US = 100)

Ireland	227.7
Switzerland	224.2
Germany	157.9
Austria	143.5
Spain	143.3
Turkey	132.4
Italy	127.0
Netherlands	124.7
France	120.9
Hungary	120.3
Belgium	109.5
UK	108.6
Slovak Republic	102.0
Poland	101.8
Finland	89.3
Russia	10.3

Source: IEA/OECD energy statistics, 1994

Reproduced by permission of the OECD

As with electricity prices, gas prices in Europe are generally well in excess of those in the US

either expanding their gas networks or, in the case of Portugal and Greece, investigating introducing natural gas using imported supplies.

In Eastern Europe, gas has traditionally been consumed mainly for district heat/power plants

Exhibit 10.9: International trade in natural gas, 1993 (billion cubic metres)

	Denmark	Germany	N'lands	Norway	UK	FSU*	Iran	Libya	Algeria	Total imports
Austria	–	0.1	–	–	–	5.3	–	–	–	5.4
Belgium	–	–	4.1	3.7	–	–	–	–	4.3	12.1
Finland	–	–	–	–	–	3.1	–	–	–	3.1
France	–	–	5.0	5.6	–	11.6	–	–	9.0	31.2
Germany	0.8	–	27.2	8.5	0.1	25.7	–	–	–	62.3
Italy	–	–	5.4	–	–	13.7	–	–	13.9	33.0
Luxembourg	–	0.7	–	–	–	–	–	–	–	0.7
Netherlands	–	–	–	2.7	0.1	–	–	–	–	2.8
Spain	–	–	–	0.2	–	–	–	1.6	4.3	6.1
Sweden	0.8	–	–	–	–	–	–	–	–	0.8
Switzerland	–	1.4	0.7	–	–	0.3	–	–	–	2.4
Turkey	–	–	–	–	–	5.0	–	–	–	5.0
UK	–	–	–	4.0	–	–	–	–	–	4.0
FSU*	–	–	–	–	–	–	0.5	–	–	0.5
Bulgaria	–	–	–	–	–	4.8	–	–	–	4.8
Czech Republic and Slovakia	–	–	–	–	–	13.3	–	–	–	13.3
Hungary	–	–	–	–	–	5.3	–	–	–	5.3
Poland	–	–	–	–	–	5.9	–	–	–	5.9
Romania	–	–	–	–	–	4.6	–	–	–	4.6
Others	–	–	–	–	–	2.3	–	–	0.3	2.6
Total Exports	**1.6**	**1.5**	**43.1**	**24.7**	**0.2**	**100.9**	**0.5**	**1.6**	**31.8**	**205.9**

* Former Soviet Union. Source: *BP Statistical Review of World Energy* 1994

Exhibit 10.10: Water costs for industrial clients, 1993 (US$ per cubic metre)

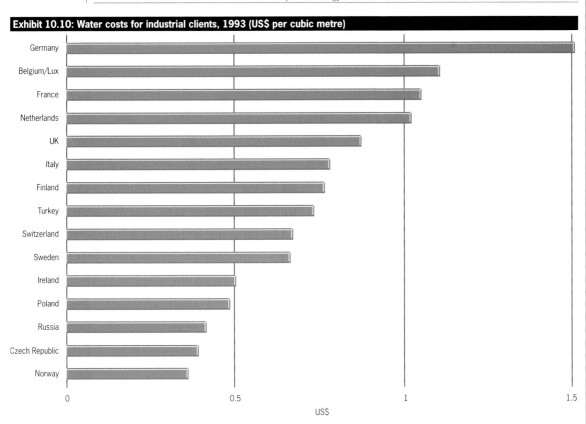

Source: IMD/World Economic Forum, 1994

Ukraine's non-payment for gas supplies has on occasion resulted in Russian threats to stop supplying

and industry. The decline of heavy industry in the region has, therefore, caused a marked drop in gas consumption. The fact that most countries in the region are heavily reliant on Russian imports is a cause of some concern, especially since the majority of exported Russian gas has to transit Ukraine. Ukraine and Russia have had considerable difficulties agreeing payment schedules, and on a number of occasions Ukraine's non-payment for gas supplies has resulted in Russian threats to stop supplying. To give themselves greater security of supply, some Eastern European countries have begun building additional storage facilities.

For the former Eastern bloc countries, liberalisation has led to a rise in energy prices as previously controlled and heavily subsidised tariffs have been replaced by prices that reflect real costs.

In Europe generally, there is a move away from standard national tariffs towards negotiated contracts which take account of transport costs.

Water

Water costs for industrial users vary across Europe by a sometimes surprising amount. In many cases, however, large industrial users are able to negotiate lower prices.

Chapter 11

FINANCIAL INCENTIVES

Financial incentives can play a significant part in determining the location of international investments. Companies tend to view the availability or lack of incentives in one of four ways:
● Only regions that offer financial incentives will be shortlisted;
● Though not essential, the offer of financial incentives plays an important part in making a company feel welcome in a new location, and is therefore expected;
● If a region offers incentives, it is regarded as a bonus, and may sway the decision in that location's favour assuming all other things are equal;
● If a region has to offer incentives then it must have significant problems and will therefore not be considered.

This chapter examines the range of financial incentives potentially available to the inward investor. Financial incentives can take many forms: grants; loans, including low interest or non-secured; tax exemptions; and low or zero cost provision of land, buildings or machinery.

The rationale for offering incentives essentially takes two forms:
● As a vehicle for the reversal of economic decline;
● To provide a 'level playing field'.

A vehicle for the reversal of economic decline
Along with the development of indigenous business, inward investment is seen as a key method of reversing the vicious circle of economic/industrial decline (see Exhibit 11.1). Attracting inward investment breaks this vicious circle of decline leading, it is hoped, to a virtuous circle (see Exhibit 11.2).

Financial incentives are therefore used to attract investment from outside the region in order to offset the lack of indigenous investment.

The level playing field
The 'level playing field' argument calls for incentives only to compensate for those being offered in other countries or regions. Naturally, if all regions offered the same level of incentives, then the overall pattern of inward investment would be identical to the pattern produced if no region offered incentives. Whether incentives do in fact attract additional investment to a region or whether the investment would have gone ahead anyway is an issue that has been hotly debated for years. Although the debate still rages today, the fact that most countries offer incentives indicates that, to most minds, the issue is clear cut: incentives attract inward investment.

Types of incentive
The type of incentive offered is often a determinant of several factors:
● Available budgets;
● Nature of investment sought by the region/country;
● Sophistication/experience of development agency/host country;
● Profile of host region.

Infrastructure provision
An alternative to payments direct to the inward investor is the provision and/or improvement of infrastructure. This is particularly attractive in areas or sites at the periphery, isolated from the main regional, national or European markets. By improving infrastructure in the form of transport, provision of utilities, access to training and business support mechanisms, the effect of geographical isolation can be reduced.

Infrastructure often degenerates in areas suffering from sectoral decline, with large industrial sites lying vacant following disinvestment. This adds to the declining appearance of a region and

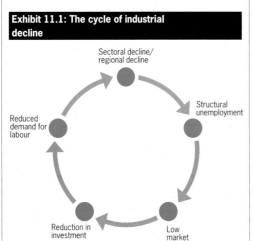

Exhibit 11.1: The cycle of industrial decline

Sectoral decline/ regional decline → Structural unemployment → Low market demand → Reduction in investment → Reduced demand for labour →

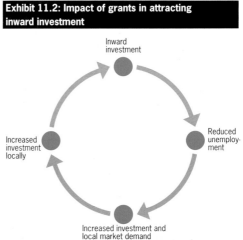

Exhibit 11.2: Impact of grants in attracting inward investment

Inward investment → Reduced unemployment → Increased investment and local market demand → Increased investment locally →

Inward investment is seen as a key method of reversing the vicious circle of economic decline

Exhibit 11.3: Advantages/disadvantages of particular types of incentives

Type	Advantages	Disadvantages
Automatic capital investment grants/automatic tax breaks	Visible, easy to understand, straightforward to administer	High proportion of 'dead weight'* Can be very expensive
Discretionary capital investment grants/ discretionary tax breaks	Reduces 'dead weight'* Cost effective. Fairly visible	Can involve lengthy evaluation. Difficult to give offers indicative before a full appraisal
Soft loans	Funds can be recycled, reduces overall budget	Not attractive to the large investor. Costly to administer
Provision of assets	Tailored to project need	Discouraged by European Commission

* 'Dead weight' = grants provided to projects that would have taken place without support

undoubtedly gives a poor image to potential investors. Infrastructure grants to local or regional authorities allow them to upgrade vacant sites, in addition to providing the infrastructural support that is likely to appeal to investors.

The role of the European Commission

It is in the field of infrastructure that grants from the European Commission have their greatest

Exhibit 11.4: Details of NGE limits currently operating

Country	Total assisted area population coverage %	Max EC aid ceiling* (NGE) %
Belgium	33	20
Denmark	20	25
France	39	25
Germany	48	23
Greece	100	75
Ireland	100	75
Italy	35	75
Luxembourg	100	25
Netherlands	20	75
Portugal	100	75
Spain	55	75
UK:		
Great Britain	35	30
Northern Ireland	100	75

* Net Grant Equivalent (NGE): the maximum grant (after tax) permitted as a percentage of capital expenditure. NGE limits may be lower in certain parts of the assisted areas. Source: EPRC

impact. The Commission has two distinct roles in the field of incentives: first, as a provider of grants and loans itself, and second, as a co-ordinator and controller of member state programmes.

The European Commission provides incentives in five main areas:

● Infrastructure and economic development;
● Agriculture and fisheries support;
● Education and training;
● Research and development;
● Special initiatives.

Infrastructure and economic development support is in the form of the Structural Funds. These are major sums of money allocated to regions (the budget provisions for 1994-99 amount to Ecu13.5 billion). Unfortunately for the private sector, almost all these budgets are paid direct to public authorities in the member states to carry out projects. Each project must have a financial contribution from the member state public sector in order to 'draw down' the EC funding.

However, the Commission does make loans available at relatively low interest rates to the private sector, in those areas suffering significant decline in the coal or steel sectors. For investment projects that create at least two jobs in the designated areas, loans meeting 50 per cent of project costs are offered at a rate of interest that can be lower than normal commercial rates. Interest

rates can be fixed or variable for the loan period, with a capital repayment holiday for the first four years. An interest rebate of 3 per cent is awarded during the first five years for a proportion of the loan, depending on the number of jobs created by the project. Loans are administered on behalf of the ECSC (European Coal and Steel Community) by major banks and other financial institutions.

The specified period for this scheme is eight years. However, the European Coal and Steel Community Treaty is due to end in 2002. As a result, repayment timescales are being steadily reduced and many financial institutions are changing the way they administer the scheme. As 2002 approaches, the future of ECSC loans is not clear: their operation may be transferred to another European institution, such as the European Investment Bank, or they may be phased out.

The second role played by the Commission is to co-ordinate the various programmes operated by member states and to ensure that these programmes abide by strict rules designed to prevent abuse of state aids, that is, any form of aid from the public to the private sector. State aids are only permitted if the incentive is provided to offset the problems of a particular region or sector.

Essentially, all member state support programmes must be submitted to the Commission for approval. The Commission lays down, in addition, general rules on the designation of assisted area status and the level of grant, as a percentage of expenditure, that can be given to projects in these areas (the so-called net grant equivalent, NGE, limits). As a restriction on the amount of grant paid towards capital expenditure, the NGE limit applies only to capital items. Grants for revenue expenditure, such as training and recruitment, are not normally included in the limit calculations.

National incentives

Provided that EC requirements are met, member states are free to offer the level and type of incentives they see fit. Although programmes differ, the main criteria influencing whether an investment will qualify for assistance and the likely level of that assistance are common. These are:

● Job creation;
● Capital expenditure;
● Environmental impact;
● Regional/national benefit from the project;
● Skill/technology content.

It is fairly straightforward to determine the criteria of the various incentives schemes, though it is far harder to reach a realistic expectation of grant. Maximum levels of grant are published, as are the European limits, where they differ. These figures can, however, lead to an over-optimistic appraisal of grant potential, as the average grant figure may well be lower. Nevertheless, member

Infrastructure grants to local or regional authorities allow them to upgrade the appearance of vacant sites

73

Exhibit 11.5: Capital investment grants across Europe

Country	Main scheme	Maximum grant % of capital investment	Comments
Austria	Loan scheme	n/a	Loans up to 50% of capital expenditure. General tax allowances including 20% for capital expenditure
Belarus	n/a	n/a	No incentives
Belgium	Capital grant	21	Covers 36.3% of population, mainly in the south of Belgium
Bulgaria	n/a	n/a	No incentives, however joint-venture income is tax-exempt for 5 years in free-trade zones and subsequently is subject to 20% tax
Croatia	Tax allowances	n/a	Exemption of tax on profits during the first year of operation; 50% reduction of tax liability during the second year and 25% for the third year. Foreign investments in special under-developed areas have a 2-year tax holiday
Czech Republic	n/a	n/a	No incentives
Denmark	n/a	n/a	No scheme in operation at the moment. Legal powers are still available to award grant in exceptional cases
Estonia	Tax allowances	n/a	3-year tax holiday and 50% tax reduction for the subsequent 5 years if foreign investment is 50% or more of statutory capital and exceeds US$1 million; if FI is more than 30% of capital and exceeds US$50,000, a 2-year tax holiday and 50% tax reduction for subsequent 2 years are applicable; if FI constitutes more than 30% of firm's statutory capital and the latter operates in a designated sector, it enjoys a 3-year tax holiday and 50% tax reduction for subsequent 2 years
Finland	Discretionary capital grants	n/a	Up to 75% of training costs related to a new investment. Other discretionary grants depending on location. Additionally, contributions can be made to training costs (up to 75%) and various tax allowances are also available
France	Regional Policy Grant	25	Covers 42% of population for manufacturing projects but much wider coverage for R&D or headquarter projects
Germany	Investment grant	23	Grants more generous in former GDR. Covers all of former GDR and 22% of former FRG
Greece	Investment grant	55	Scheme due to be overhauled. Currently covers 58% of population and excludes Athens
Hungary	n/a	n/a	No incentives
Ireland	New ind programme	60	One of a combination of similar programmes available all over Ireland
Italy	Assistance for Regional Development Areas	50	Scheme not yet operational due to delays in legislation. Will be targeted at SMEs in northern areas and all firms in the south
Latvia	Tax allowances	n/a	Automatic tax allowances with discretionary top-up. 2-year tax holiday starting in first year of tax generation. 50% reduction in profit tax in subsequent 2 years. If investment exceeds US$1 million, the tax holiday is extended to 3 years and 50% reduction for next 5 years
Lithuania	Tax allowances	n/a	If FTE is registered before 31 December 1993, foreign share of profits enjoys a 70% tax reduction for the first 5 years after the first income is declared and a 50% tax reduction for the subsequent 3 years; if FTE is registered between 1 January 1994 and 31 December 1995, foreign share of profits enjoys a 50% tax reduction for 6 years
Luxembourg	Regional assistance for investment	25	Discretionary capital grant
Netherlands	Investment premium	20	Grant is automatic up to US$2 million expenditure. Discretion to award higher grants for larger projects
Norway	Industrial and Regional Development Fund	n/a	Loans available but usually only on normal business terms
Poland	Tax allowances	n/a	3 year tax-free period for foreign investment was automatic, but is now discretionary, targeted at major investments in priority sectors and high unemployment areas
Portugal	Regional aid system	70% combination of grant + loan	The scheme has very recently been introduced. It is directed at mainland Portugal excluding the coastal areas between Braga and Setubal and between Lagos and Faro
Romania	Tax allowances	n/a	Various tax incentives
Russian Federation	Tax allowances	n/a	General tax holiday for investments now at an end. 1-year tax reductions for firms investing in priority and designated sectors are possible; JVs registered after 1 January 1994, engaged in production activities and having at least 30% paid-in foreign share in capitalisation (worth at least US$10 million) enjoy a 2-year tax holiday; during the subsequent 2 years, profit tax rate does not exceed $1/4$ or $1/2$ of the average tax rate
Slovakia	n/a	n/a	No major incentives
Spain	Regional Investment Grant	75	Covers 55% of country excluding Madrid and north west areas
Sweden	Location grant, development grant and employment grant	70	Assisted areas cover 60% of country but only 8% of population
Switzerland	Federal schemes	n/a	Vary enormously between cantons. Can include up to 10 years' tax-free period or cheap land/buildings
UK: Great Britain	Regional Selective Assistance	30	Vital to demonstrate credibly the need for assistance. Covers 35% of population
Northern Ireland	Industrial Development Grant	50	Maximum grant is 30% but an additional 20% is available for inward investment projects. Scheme is similar to Great Britain's RSA
Ukraine	Tax allowances	n/a	5-year tax holiday for companies with foreign equity share exceeding 20% and worth at least US$50,000; if foreign equity share is 30% or more. The firm enjoys a 5-year tax holiday and 30% tax reduction subsequently

states are normally very receptive to inward investors, and so the actual level to the inward investor is frequently above the average.

Applying for grants: additionality meets viability

Automatic grant schemes are becoming hard to find. Though administratively simpler, automatic schemes by definition give grants to projects that would have gone ahead without assistance of this kind; a proportion of the grant budget is therefore wasted on so-called 'dead-weight' projects. A project has *additionality* if the grant is an essential component of the funding package. Discretionary incentives are designed to ensure that all projects have an element of additionality.

It is frequently the case, then, that investors have to demonstrate a need for a grant. Clearly in the case of small firms this can most easily be done by demonstrating a shortage of funds or a cashflow deficit. For larger firms, the shortage of funds argument may not be appropriate, but it can be argued that, without a grant, the project fails to meet a pay-back or rate-of-return requirement imposed at group level. For inward investment projects, it is often by costing competing locations, including incentive packages available, that a case for grant can be made.

Applicants also need to demonstrate that both they and the project are viable. This will ensure that jobs created will be maintained for a reasonable time. For large firms this is not usually a problem, though guarantees are often requested from holding or parent companies.

Administrative details vary widely but there are two golden rules which apply to most schemes:
● Do not start the project until you have discussed it with the grant providers. Prior commitment means no grant at all in the UK, based on the argument that if investors start the project before knowing whether a grant would be provided, they do not really need one. In France, Belgium and Spain, investors must at least lodge an application before starting;
● Do not promise the earth. Failure to deliver the jobs and expenditure outlined in the application can lead to repayment of the grant, and 'clawback' penalties may be severe.

Most grant schemes are discretionary. From a government point of view, this means that money can be targeted at particularly beneficial projects and acts as a money-saving practice which allows grants to be withheld from projects that would have proceeded anyway. Discretionary grant schemes can, however, cause problems for the inward investor, making it difficult to establish exactly what would be forthcoming for a particular project. Most discretionary schemes require detailed applications to be completed, making a case for a grant to the authorities.

As well as wishing to satisfy itself that a grant is necessary, the grant authority will also be influenced by the number and type of jobs created by the project, the industry involved, the level and nature of investment, and the wider benefits to the region. Some years ago the scale of inward investment in Europe led a number of people to question the long-term benefits. In particular, some argued that if investment consisted of assembly plants, with HQ staff, administration and research functions all remaining in the home country, there could be a long term de-skilling of

the host country. For this reason grant agencies are particularly well disposed to projects that create 'quality' jobs, that is, skilled manual and senior management jobs in addition to non-skilled positions.

The counter-argument to this insistence on quality jobs is that the unemployed in assisted areas are predominantly unskilled or semi-skilled; 'quality' inward investment is therefore less likely to bring them into the labour market than, for example, assembly jobs.

Incentives in Eastern Europe

A number of incentives are available to attract inward investment into various Eastern European countries. The autonomy of each incentive scheme has led to a wide divergence in availability, but some interesting patterns are emerging.

Inward investment has traditionally been limited in the Eastern European region due to trade and currency conversion restrictions and the general non-capitalist environment. Those companies that did invest were sometimes offered one-off 'gifts' of land, buildings or grants. For the authorities concerned, the cost per project could be high, but was so rare as not to cause budgetary problems. As economies have been liberalised they have been actively seeking to attract investment and offering incentives. However, the lack of funds available and the absence of a developed business support structure has led to tax incentives being offered, on an automatic basis, for capital projects, rather than grants.

Certain Eastern European countries have opted for a totally free market approach. For example, the Czech Republic has declared its opposition to all forms of incentives, while at the same time welcoming inward investment openly.

Grant combinations

Incentives are frequently offered from several sources in the same country. The usual pattern is that there is one regional incentive scheme, available from a national ministry – for example the Department of Trade and Industry in the UK or DATAR in France. This may be supplemented by local aid schemes such as grants for building adaptations or refurbishments offered at a regional level. Local schemes may also include training assistance or management development grants.

Several grants, loans, and so on can be given to the same project, though the total package should not exceed NGE limits in EU member states. However, certain grants towards revenue expenditure items such as training may not have to be included in the NGE total.

It is worth noting that the first discussions companies have concerning incentives for investment will not necessarily be with the people who have the real power to give grants. Inward investment agencies are often separate from the grant providers and, as such, are not always in the best position to make indicative offers.

In conclusion

As membership of the European Union widens, the new member states will find it necessary to conform to the Commission's constraints on state aid, expressed through NGE limits. However, the ability and desire of member states to offer incentives are likely to remain for some time across most of Europe.

Chapter 12

TRANSPORT

With road transport levels forecast to rise inexorably, the choice has to be made whether to increase road provision or reduce the total amount of traffic

Transport is a key location factor for most businesses. It is obviously essential to be able to move manufactured goods from factory to market quickly and cost effectively. It is also critical to be able to access subsidiaries, parent HQ and key business contacts around Europe. Both the quality and extent of freight and passenger transport services must therefore be taken into account. This chapter examines briefly each of the major transport modes and provides comparable data for each.

The main issues affecting transport in Europe are congestion and the environment. With road traffic levels forecast to rise inexorably, the choice has to be made whether to increase road provision or in some way reduce the total amount of traffic. Both approaches are fraught with political difficulty. It is clear, however, that in the long term, road pricing in the form of tolls will be introduced widely throughout Europe, and measures will be taken to stem the increase in road traffic. For manufacturing companies, this is likely to have one of two effects: increases in transport costs may mean a move away from just-in-time (JIT) production, with its dependence on regular deliveries, towards holding higher levels of stocks; or, as congestion decreases as private cars are priced off the road, firms may move to even tighter JIT production methods.

For the business traveller, the increasing sophistication of telecommunications may result in a reduced need for travel as video conferencing becomes more common. However, such changes will take time to develop and, in the short term at least, travellers in Europe can look forward to increasingly congested skies and roads.

For freight, the mode of transport used across Europe varies considerably depending on the type of goods being moved, available infrastructure and topography. As Exhibit 12.1 illustrates, most cross-border freight is moved by sea and road. Railways are important in Eastern Europe, while inland waterways are heavily used in those countries where they are available. For national traffic, the road network becomes even more

important, though once again, railways are still heavily used in Eastern Europe.

Air transport

Air traffic, both passenger and freight, continues to grow at a rapid rate, leading to increased congestion and delays. The result is massive investment in new infrastructure and a hope that

Exhibit 12.2: Percentage of national freight carried by mode (tonne km)

	Road	Water	Rail
Albania	65.9	19.9	32.2
Armenia	13.1		86.9
Austria	30.8	27.8	41.3
Belgium	67.3	12.8	19.9
Bulgaria	59.1		40.9
Croatia	47.8	7.8	44.3
Czech Republic	19.3	3.8	76.9
Denmark	79.4	12.2	8.4
Estonia	20.3		79.7
Finland	66.8	8.0	25.1
France	74.5	3.1	22.4
Germany	59.9	16.3	23.8
Greece	93.4		6.6
Hungary	18.1	27.6	54.2
Ireland	89.1		10.9
Italy	89.1		10.9
Latvia	14.7		85.3
Lithuania	38.3		61.3
Macedonia	71.2		28.8
Moldova	32.4		67.4
Netherlands	78.9	18.1	3.0
Norway	41.6	48.9	9.4
Poland	46.8	0.5	52.7
Portugal	87.2		12.8
Romania	35.2	3.9	60.9
Slovenia	51.8	27.3	20.9
Spain	93.5		6.5
Sweden	52.9	14.2	32.8
Switzerland	55.6	44.4	
Turkey	92.4		7.6
UK	89.3	0.1	10.6
Ukraine	16.9	1.9	81.3

Figures may not add up to 100 due to rounding. Source: UN *Annual Bulletin of Transport Statistics for Europe* 1994

Exhibit 12.1: Freight model share for selected countries (percentage of total import/exports by weight carried by mode)

		Road	Rail	Inland waterway	Sea	Air	Pipeline
Belgium	imports	26.5	4.4	18.4	35.9	0.1	14.8
(1991)	exports	51.0	8.5	16.0	22.8	0.6	1.2
Denmark	imports	17.0	3.2	10.2	69.5	–	–
(1992)	exports	29.4	3.0	7.3	60.1	0.1	–
France	imports	26.6	4.5	4.4	64.3	0.1	–
(1992)	exports	42.2	12.2	10.3	35.1	0.1	–
Netherlands	imports	15.2	1.1	11.1	71.5	0.1	1.0
(1991)	exports	19.1	1.9	33.0	23.3	0.1	22.6
Romania	imports	1.3	53.3	0.3	15.7	–	29.5
(1992)	exports	4.5	71.2	1.2	15.0	0.3	7.8

Source: UN *Annual Bulletin of Transport Statistics for Europe* 1994

high-speed rail services will divert some shorter haul passengers from the skies, thereby freeing up space for growth in long-haul journeys.

The impact of liberalisation has been a rapid growth in alliances such as British Airways' Deutsche operation in Germany, or code sharing, especially between European and US carriers. The aim is that the main airlines should be able to offer global rather than national networks. The days of national carriers are surely numbered as they are replaced by a few global airlines and a larger number of smaller, niche regional operators.

The great paradox of the air transport industry is that despite rapid and almost continued growth, the majority of European national airlines are facing major financial problems. Air France, Alitalia, Aer Lingus and Olympic Airways are all major loss-makers. Even Lufthansa has only recently returned to profitability after five years of losses. Of the larger operators, only British Airways has consistently returned profits in recent years.

In Eastern Europe, many carriers have been, or are scheduled for, full or part privatisation. In some respects, they have progressed further than the West in this regard.

Continuing restructuring, privatisation and increased competition will in the short term lead to considerable uncertainty and probably further labour unrest among the national carriers. In the long run, however, passengers can expect to benefit from a more efficient and hopefully cheaper air service. (In the US, for example, fare levels are such that even the coach operators are now being undercut.) France is the latest European country to experience the effects of liberalisation, as new entrants on its domestic routes bring about intense price competition. Such changes will not, however, assist in relation to congestion and delays at major airports. Airport and airspace congestion will, it is

estimated, cost European countries US$6 billion annually by the year 2000.

Expansion plans are well under way or planned at many Eastern European airports, which have seen the largest growth in traffic. The impact of developments in Eastern Europe is illustrated by the fact that a third of customers at Vienna airport are now East European carriers, while 20 per cent of Lufthansa's German traffic is accounted for by the former GDR.

Increasing environmental concerns have delayed some expansions, and a new airport at Berlin still seems some way off. However, a number of new regional airports are being planned or developed. One factor encouraging such developments is the end of the Cold War and the subsequent availability of former military airfields. Nevertheless, the Association of European Airlines reports that delays are worsening, with up to 15 per cent of intra-European flight departures being delayed by more than 15 minutes. These delays are caused mainly by airport and air traffic control deficiencies. For example, in 1994 up to 20 per cent of flights from Budapest left late due to air traffic capacity problems in neighbouring countries – a situation that has been exacerbated by the problems in the former Yugoslavia.

The European Commission has realised that congestion will undermine new airline competition, and that if no new airlines can enter the market because of the lack of slots at key airports the industry will maintain its monopolistic position. The Commission's short-term solution is to require that all newly created, unused, vacated or otherwise free slots should be pooled, with up to half of them being allocated to new entrants. Slots will be lost by incumbents if not used for at least 80 per cent of the time.

London Heathrow remains Europe's busiest airport (although with the impact of the Channel Tunnel it will be interesting to see if Europe's

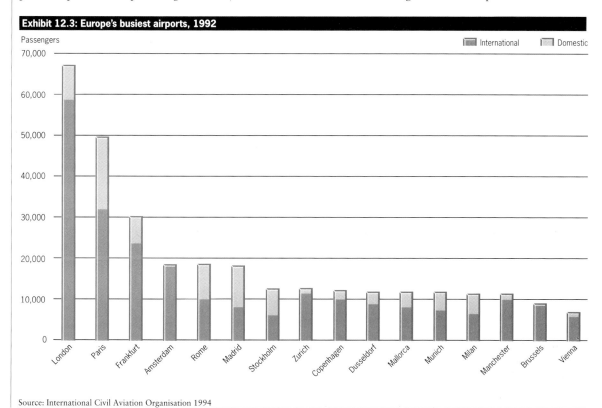

Exhibit 12.3: Europe's busiest airports, 1992

Passengers

International   Domestic

Source: International Civil Aviation Organisation 1994

The days of national carriers are surely numbered, as they are replaced by a few global airlines

Exhibit 12.4: Basic road transport indicators, 1993

	Road density (road km/km²)	Traffic congestion index (vehicles km/road km)
Italy	1,014	1,268
UK	1,575	1,237
Netherlands	2,570	945
Luxembourg	1,977	766
Sweden	331	745
Portugal	1,095	736
Germany	1,782	726
Switzerland	1,723	699*
Czech Republic	709	590
Finland	229	566
France	1,473	566
Denmark	1,650	547
Greece	880	439*
Slovenia	728	438
Belgium	4,515	423
Russia	28	368
Bulgaria	333	356
Poland	1,178	310
Spain	668	299
Moldova	430	292
Ukraine	282	288*
Ireland	1,314	279
Macedonia	327	276
Estonia	328	275*
Norway	279	251
Croatia	476	226*
Austria	2,385	216
Hungary	1,706	159
Belarus	243	129*
Lithuania	853	121*
Turkey	498	79
Latvia	1,002	56
Romania	1,937	50
Albania	642	43*
Armenia	259	39*

Source: World Road Statistics 1993, IRF 1994
* Estimate based on typical annual mileage per vehicle in other similar countries

busiest international air route, London-Paris, remains in the top place). In terms of freight handled, Frankfurt is Europe's leading airport, with London, Paris and Brussels the next most important airports.

A large volume of air freight is currently trucked between major airports, but some airlines are now considering using rail freight services instead. Lufthansa, for example, plans to bring cargo from Hamburg and northern Italy to Frankfurt by rail rather than road. This is in response to increasing road congestion which has caused cargo trucks to be held up and flights to be delayed as a result.

Road transport

Increasing congestion, environmental pressures and the need for huge infrastructural improvements are the key issues now facing road users. Road traffic continues to increase and there appears to be insufficient political will to reverse that trend.

In an attempt to overcome the problem of congestion, countries have tried, with limited success, to shift more freight to rail and water transport. There have been particular efforts to lessen freight traffic on routes from Germany into Eastern Europe, where long delays at border crossings and limited capacity on existing road networks have placed pressure on hauliers to put their trucks on piggy-back rail services.

Road traffic continues to increase and there appears to be insufficient political will to reverse that trend

The growth in increased intra-European trade is also resulting in a vast increase in transit traffic which is adding to congestion in countries such as Belgium and Germany. In an attempt to make transit traffic pay something towards the roads it uses, Germany, Belgium, the Netherlands, Denmark and Luxembourg – countries that have tended to have toll-free motorways in the past – have together established a common road-user tax on heavy goods vehicles. The charges levied, depending on a vehicle's weight and number of axles, range from Ecu6 per day up to Ecu1,250 per year. Switzerland has gone one step further: following a recent referendum, it requires that all transit traffic should be moved by rail by the year 2004 (in fact 90 per cent of such traffic already goes by this mode). Austria, which faces an increase in transit traffic of 140-230 per cent on east-west routes, may also force more traffic to go by rail or waterway.

Some companies have already switched traffic from road to rail on environmental grounds; for example, Coca-Cola has switched to rail for bulk traffic between France and Germany; Jacobs-Suchard and Necherman in Germany have also announced moves to rail transport. These developments are just a drop in the ocean, however, since the vast amount of freight continues to be moved by road. The result is severe congestion in countries such as the UK, Italy and the Netherlands, and increasingly on the over-stretched road networks of Eastern Europe.

One of the key problems faced by the road haulage industry is the number of small opera-

Exhibit 12.5: Europe's main container ports

	No. of TEGU 1992
Rotterdam	4,122,782
Hamburg	2,268,481
Antwerp	1,835,595
Felixstowe	1,542,551
Algerias	780,366
Le Havre	746,366
La Spezia	595,738
Zeebrugge	547,757
Barcelona	525,000
Piraeus	511,465
Southampton	446,562
Valencia	370,546
Gothenburg	369,973
Tilbury	368,508
Liverpool	353,285
Marseilles	350,331
Genoa	337,629
Leghorn	333,756
Lisbon	293,857
Hull	274,449
Harwich	205,468
Bilbao	204,421
Aarhus	184,000
Istanbul	179,189
Waterford	144,203
Oslo	106,095
Gdynia	97,894
St Petersburg	73,620
Kotka (Finland)	66,500
Constanta (Romania)	58,200
Ilyichevsk (Ukraine)	54,112
Koper (Slovenia)	45,834
Rijeka (Croatia)	44,563
Varna (Bulgaria)	28,649

Source: Containerisation International Yearbook 1994

Exhibit 12.6: Road freight regulations

	Road trains Length (metres)	Road trains Weight (tonnes)	Maximum motorway speed (kmph)	Weekend restrictions	Night-time restrictions
Albania	18	40	45	X	X
Austria	18	38	70	√	√
Belgium	18.35	44	90	X	X
Bulgaria	20	38	50	X	X
Croatia	18	48	70	√	X
Czech Republic	18	48	70	√	X
Denmark	18.5	44	70	X	X
Estonia	18.35	44	90	X	X
Finland	22	48	80	X	X
Former Yugoslavia	18	40	70	√	X
France	18	40	80	√	X
Germany	18.35	40	80	√	X
Greece	18	40	60	√	X
Hungary	18	40	80	X	X
Ireland	18	40	64	X	X
Italy	18	44	60	√	X
Lithuania	18.25	36	90	X	X
Luxembourg	18	40	60	X	X
Macedonia	18	48	70	√	X
Netherlands	18	50	80	X	X
Norway	18	50	70	X	X
Poland	22	38	60	X	X
Portugal	18	40	70	√	X
Romania	18.35	40	50	X	X
Russia	20	36	70	X	X
Slovakia	18	48	70	√	X
Slovenia	18	40	60	√	X
Spain	18	40	100	√	X
Sweden	24	42	70	X	X
Switzerland	18	28	80	√	√
Turkey	22	42	70	X	X
UK	18	38	96	X	X

√ indicates some restrictions. Source: Freight Transport Association/Croner's Road Transport Operation 1995

The port sector is going through considerable turmoil in parts of Europe such as France, Ireland and Italy, as major restructuring is carried out to improve efficiency

tors which survive by providing low-cost services. Increased competition has led to a growth in tachograph fraud, overloading of lorries and concern about safety standards. Larger operators in high-cost countries have started to 'flag-out' their fleets – that is, register their vehicles in lower cost countries such as Spain.

While harmonisation of the dimensions of vehicles is gradually being achieved, there remain discrepancies on weights, speed limits and weekend movement restrictions. Vehicle weights especially remain an emotive issue, with Germany recently coming out strongly against a rise to 44 tonnes. The UK, which is slowly moving to this higher level, now allows 44-tonne vehicle weights for journeys to and from rail heads for combined transport operations.

Ports, shipping and inland waterways

The port sector is going through considerable turmoil in parts of Europe such as France, Ireland and Italy, as major restructuring is carried out to improve efficiency and reduce overmanning.

The European Commission is trying to increase the level of competition and open access into this predominantly public-sector owned business. The main sea ports are located in Northern Europe, with the top four ports handling more containers than virtually all the other European ports put together. Most port traffic is international in nature, though in countries such as Spain and Sweden there is a considerable amount of national short-sea traffic. The main disadvantage of short-journey services is the high ratio of time spent in port to time spent at sea,

Exhibit 12.7: Length of navigable inland waterways and amount of freight carried, 1992

	Length (km)	Freight carried (tonne km)	Index of use (tonne km/km)
Austria	358	1,462	4.08
Belarus	2,579	990	0.38
Belgium	1,513	5,083	3.36
Bulgaria	470	837	1.78
Croatia	1,947	52	0.03
Czech Republic	4,144	2,978	0.72
Estonia	520	1	–
Finland	6,197	–	–
France	5,881	8,831	1.47
Germany	4,350	51,345	11.80
Hungary	1,464	1,495	1.02
Italy	1,366	87	0.06
Latvia	4,350	404	0.09
Lithuania	789	45	0.06
Luxembourg	37	338	9.14
Netherlands	5,046	34,798	6.90
Poland	3,805	751	0.20
Portugal	124	–	–
Moldova	622	27	0.04
Romania	1,778	1,890	1.06
Russia	97,793	135,792	1.39
Sweden	439	-	-
Switzerland	21	50	2.38
Turkey	–	305	–
Ukraine	3,748	8,217	2.19
UK	1,192	200	0.17

Source: UN Transport Statistics, Europe 1994

though this problem may be resolved with the introduction of new technology such as self-loading/unloading vessels. These developments

The vast amount of freight continues to be moved by road. The result is severe congestion in countries such as the UK, Italy and the Netherlands

could allow regular services with vessels operating on specific 'bus' routes, picking up and setting down traffic at regular stops.

Despite the environmental benefits and the success of developments like the new Rhine-Danube canal (which is carrying more traffic than expected, even with the continuing problems in the former Yugoslavia), the inland waterways of Europe face considerable difficulties, due in part to the economic recession and the continued decline of heavy industry in Europe.

The waterways of Germany, the Netherlands and Austria are still heavily used, while vast volumes of freight are carried on Russia's extensive inland waterway network (though the collapse of heavy industry in Russia will no doubt have greatly reduced this figure recently). But in general the sector is suffering from over-capacity and intense competition from parts of Eastern Europe. Problems have arisen, for example, because of competition from Polish barges which have undercut German traffic on the River Oder.

The future is perhaps brighter, with a number of new developments planned. These include a navigable north-south waterway running through the Czech and Slovak republics which would enable traffic to travel from Vienna through Bratislava to Poland. A Rhine-Rhône canal is also planned in France at a cost of Ecu2.5 billion.

Germany has moved towards establishing a number of combined freight-traffic centres utilising road, rail and inland waterways. In their most advanced form, these centres would enable not only the transfer of goods between modes but also repackaging, labelling and even some basic assembly.

Railways

Despite being seen as environmentally friendly, European railways are facing considerable difficulties. Although new high-speed routes have been extremely successful, total passenger traffic is at best static, while freight continues to decline. Combined transport is seen as one possible saviour of the railways; the other is privatisation. The UK and the Netherlands lead the way in this respect, while Germany is opening its rail network to open freight access.

The railways need massive investment in new rolling stock and infrastructure, but at the same time they are often saddled with loss-making routes which, for political reasons they cannot close. As a result, few of them have the resources to undertake the necessary investment. The railways in Eastern Europe, which in the past were often profitable, have suffered from massive under-investment; as heavy industry has collapsed and coach services have been liberalised, new traffic levels have fallen by more than two-thirds in some cases.

Throughout Europe, limited moves have been made towards privatisation while significant

The railways are often saddled with loss-making routes which, for political reasons, they cannot close

Exhibit 12.8: Passenger and freight traffic on European railways in 1993

	Passenger journeys 1993 (millions)	Passenger km 1993 (millions)	Average journey length 1993 (km)	Freight tonnes 1993 (millions)	Freight tonne km 1993 (millions)	Average haul (km)
Armenia	1.3*	400*	307.7	2.5*	4,200*	1,680.0
Austria	181.1	9,342	51.6	60.3	11,798	195.7
Azerbaijan	9.0	1,200	133.3	18.3	7,300	298.9
Belarus	182.8	19,500	106.7	71.5	42,900	600.0
Belgium	145.8	6,798	46.9	62.3	8,074	129.6
Bulgaria	76.1	6,837	89.9	31.4	7,702	245.2
Croatia	19.7	1,034	52.5	11.6	1,663	143.4
Czech Republic	242.2	8,548	35.3	125.2	23,750	189.7
Denmark	139.7	4,598	35.3	125.2	1,797	210.3
Estonia	16.7	722.4	43.3	24.2	3,743	154.5
Finland	44.4	3,007	67.7	37.9	9,259	244.3
France	813.1	58,209	71.6	118.4	44,400	375.0
Georgia	5.8*	1,200*	206.9	3.4	1,600	296.3
Germany	1426.2	56,530	39.6	314.4	64,600	205.5
Greece	12.2	2,046	167.6	3.4	803	236.4
Hungary	158.5	8,438	53.2	43.5	7,451	171.4
Ireland	26.1	1,274	48.7	3.1	574	187.7
Italy	438.3	47,106	107.5	59.9	18,791	313.7
Latvia	59.6	2,359	39.6	30.6	9,852	322.2
Lithuania	24.8	2,700	108.9	38.4	11,030	287.2
Luxembourg	–	–	–	17.4	647	37.3
Moldova	14.9*	1,500*	100.7	9.1*	7,700*	846.2
Netherlands	333.0	15,200	45.7	16.7	2,700	161.7
Norway	37.5	2,316	61.8	20.3	2,368	303.6
Poland	448.9	24,782	55.1	208.3	63,246	303.6
Portugal	172.6	4,471	25.9	6.8	1,539	226.6
Russia	2,300.0	271,600	118.1	1,344.3	1,615,000	1,201.4
Romania	225.4	19,402	86.1	98.1	21,871	222.9
Serbia	31.5	2,965	91.0	5.7	1,699	143.4
Slovakia	86.7	4,569	52.7	64.8	13,916	214.8
Spain	353.5	15,457	43.7	19.1	7,497	392.5
Sweden	92.7	5,830	62.9	51.4	18,568	361.2
Switzerland	263.8	12,000	45.5	44.1	7,329	166.2
UK	718.9	30,549	42.5	103.3	13,764	133.2
Ukraine	491.6*	76,200*	155.0	735.4	337,700*	459.2

* 1992 data. Source: *Railway Gazette International* 1994

The rail
systems of
the former
Soviet Union
are massive
compared
with those
in the West

TRANSPORT

Exhibit 12.9: Percentage of passenger trains arriving on time or within margin indicated (1992 or 1993 data)

		%			%
Armenia	All services (0 mins)	63.9	Latvia	Long distance (10 mins)	95.9
Azerbaijan	All services (0 mins)	79.9	Lithuania	Long distance (5 mins)	96.9
Belarus	All services (0 mins)	94.8	Luxembourg	All services (n/a)	85.1
Belgium	All services (5 mins)	92.6	Moldova	All services (0 mins)	94.2
Bulgaria	Long distance (5 mins)	91.5	Netherlands	Long distance (5 mins)	97.1
Denmark	Long distance (5 mins)	84	Norway	Long distance (5 mins)	79
Estonia	Long distance (n/a)	86.3	Poland	Long distance (5 mins)	89.7
Finland	Long distance (5 mins)	91.5	Russia	All services (0 mins)	97.3
France	Long distance (14 mins)	94.5	Spain	All services (10 mins)	87.5
Georgia	All services (0 mins)	56.7	Sweden	Long distance (5 mins)	78
Germany	Inter-city (5 mins)	84.7	Switzerland	All services (5 mins)	95
Hungary	Long distance (0 mins)	74.7	UK	Inter-city (10 mins)	90.6
Ireland	Long distance (9 mins)	62	Ukraine	All services (0 mins)	87.2
Italy	Long distance (15 mins)	84			

Source: *Railway Gazette International* 1994. Figures in brackets indicate margin of lateness

Exhibit 12.10: Basic railway infrastructure

	Rail density (km/km^2) x 1,000	% electrified	Traffic density traffic km/length of rail network
Russia	5.2	4.35	21.5
Ukraine	51.6	36.9	18.3
Belarus	26.8	15.9	11.4
Lithuania	30.7	6.1	8.5
Moldova	39.3	0	6.9
Netherlands	66.9	72.2	6.5
Switzerland	78.2	99.5	6.0
Armenia	27.9		5.5
Latvia	37.3	11.3	5.1
Estonia	22.6	13.0	4.4
Belgium	112.5	66.8	4.3
Italy	53.5	61.7	4.1
Austria	66.8	57.9	3.8
Romania	47.9	33.1	3.6
Poland	80.8	45.5	3.5
Bulgaria	38.7	61.7	3.4
France	59.4	39.7	3.1
Germany	114.3	40.4	3.0
UK	67.4	29.7	2.9
Denmark	53.5	12.1	2.8
Czech Republic	157.0	30.3	2.6
Sweden	23.9	73.8	2.5
Luxembourg	106.0	80.0	2.4
Hungary	83.1	29.8	2.1
Albania	23.4	0.0	2.0
Portugal	34.4	15.1	2.0
Finland	19.3	28.3	1.9
Spain	25.8	52.9	1.8
Norway	12.4	60.2	1.2
Greece	18.8	0.0	1.1
Croatia	47.5	35.9	1.0
Ireland	27.7	1.9	0.9
Slovenia		41.5	–
Turkey	10.4	10.7	–

Source: Ernst & Young *Annual Bulletin of Transport Statistics for Europe* 1994/World
Road Statistics IRF, 1994/*Railway Gazette International* 1994

rationalisations have been taking place. In the long term, Europe's railways are likely to experience continuing rationalisation, with priority being given to major inter-city services and combined freight.

A gradual development is the move towards a common gauge for rolling stock throughout Europe. Spain, for example, has built a new high-speed line from Madrid to Seville on the standard European gauge and is planning to convert some of its other main lines to the standard gauge. The Baltic states are considering moving from Russia's broad gauge to the European standard gauge because they see their future as being with the West rather than the East.

Even though most of them have now lost half their traffic, the rail systems of the former Soviet Union are massive compared with those in the West. In the long term, there is a great potential for a private freight railway system similar to that operating in the US.

The quality of rail services varies considerably between countries. Those in Georgia and Armenia have been badly affected by internal fighting while Russia still appears to be able to run its trains on time.

Chapter 13

THE ENVIRONMENT

The environment is increasingly recognised as an important factor to take into account when making business investment and location decisions. Several aspects are commonly considered by companies when assessing locations. These include:

● *The availability of natural resources and the quality of the natural environment:* The availability of water, land and other natural resources may be a key consideration in deciding on the site for a new plant, as these can represent a high proportion of raw material costs and can affect operational factors. Air quality is a particularly noticeable facet influencing the quality of life;

● *The regulatory and institutional framework:* National and European Union laws and other international agreements have created a sizeable legislative agenda for most European countries. The result of these measures is a degree of uniformity in approach to environmental regulation, but significant scope for variation remains;

● *Regional and national priorities for action:* Countries have different national priorities, reflecting their geography, geology, historical land use, socio-economic conditions, political culture, level of infrastructure development, industrial history and so on;

● *Levels of public interest in environmental matters:* The preparedness of the public to object to a new development on environmental grounds – or more positively, to buy environment-friendly products – can have a very significant bearing on company activity. Pressure group activity has also had a significant effect on corporate marketing, sales strategies and public relations efforts.

Every location or investment decision will combine a range of these factors in a unique way. Businesses are well advised to weigh them all carefully. This chapter examines each of the four main areas of concern outlined above.

Natural resources and the natural environment
Judgements about the quality of the natural environment need to be taken in the local context, as conditions can vary markedly even within very close geographical areas. An indication of the state of the natural environment in a range of European locations is provided below, based on a selection of the many indicators of air, water and land quality.

Exhibit 13.1: Emissions to air – percentage reduction per capita since 1980

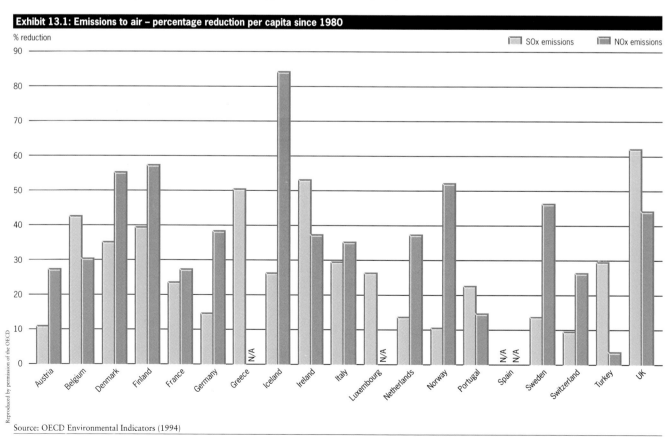

Source: OECD Environmental Indicators (1994)

The preparedness of the public to buy environment-friendly products can have a very significant bearing on company activity

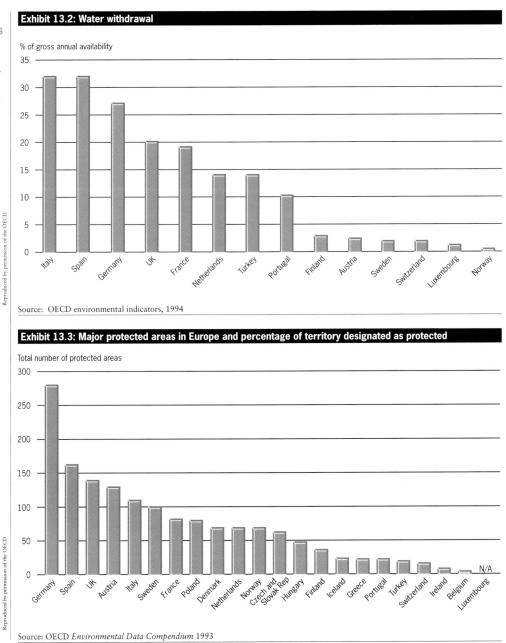

Reproduced by permission of the OECD

Exhibit 13.2: Water withdrawal

% of gross annual availability

Source: OECD environmental indicators, 1994

Exhibit 13.3: Major protected areas in Europe and percentage of territory designated as protected

Total number of protected areas

Source: OECD *Environmental Data Compendium* 1993

Exhibit 13.4: Waste treatment capacity

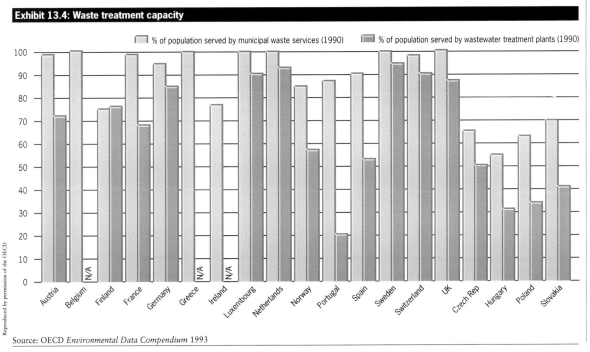

□ % of population served by municipal waste services (1990)   □ % of population served by wastewater treatment plants (1990)

Reproduced by permission of the OECD

Source: OECD *Environmental Data Compendium* 1993

Pressure group activity has had a significant effect on corporate marketing, sales strategies and public relations efforts

83

Exhibit 13.5: Recycling rates (1990)

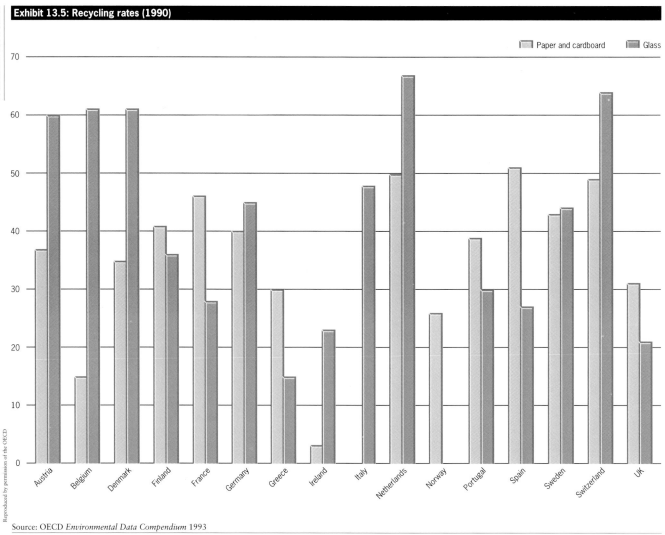

Paper and cardboard   Glass

Source: OECD *Environmental Data Compendium* 1993

In many
Southern
and Eastern
European
areas, good
quality water
is not readily
available
without
investment in
purification
and
treatment

Air

Man-made emissions of sulphur dioxide and nitrogen oxide (so-called SOx and NOx emissions), which arise principally from energy utilities, combustion processes and vehicles, are two important indicators of environmental quality. Emission levels obviously reflect a particular region's industrial development, historical patterns of power generation, the degree of vehicle ownership and so on.

Per capita emissions of both SOx and NOx are shown in Exhibit 13.1. Every country listed has achieved reductions (in absolute levels) of SOx emissions since 1980. Germany, Austria and Sweden have achieved reductions of more than 70 per cent, while Portugal and Ireland have achieved far lower levels of 21 per cent and 15 per cent respectively. The trends in NOx emissions are far less positive, with increased emission levels in Denmark, Finland, Iceland, Ireland, Italy, Norway and the UK.

Water

The availability of water – often an important factor for industrial plant location – is also an issue of growing environmental significance. In many Southern and Eastern European areas, good quality water is not readily available without investment in purification and treatment. As well as water quality, water availability is also a fundamental consideration, since excessive water consumption may prove unsustainable. (Exhibit

13.2 illustrates water withdrawal as a percentage of gross annual availability.)

In countries where water withdrawal levels have increased since 1980 (such as France, the UK, Germany, Portugal and Turkey), the pressure to increase water prices or promote conservation measures may be felt more intensely in future.

Land use/land quality

A significant issue for businesses making location decisions is the quality of the land. This is an issue that has gained in importance because of the potential for inheriting contamination in previously used industrial sites and premises. Estimates of the degree of contamination across Europe's regions are difficult to make because of ignorance of past land-use or contaminative activities, and inconsistency in definitions of what constitutes contamination. It is clear, however, that all long-established European urban industrial areas have inherited problems of contaminated land. These problems are particularly acute in Eastern European countries where military, nuclear and power utility sites have been poorly controlled.

Protecting unspoilt land and natural ecosystems from development is therefore a key objective for many countries, and the pressures on governments to safeguard bio-diversity is of growing importance, particularly in view of the Rio summit's Convention on Biological Diversity. Exhibit 13.3 shows the number of designated protected

Exhibit 13.6: Progress in implementing environmental directives, 1993 (percentage of directives for which measures notified)

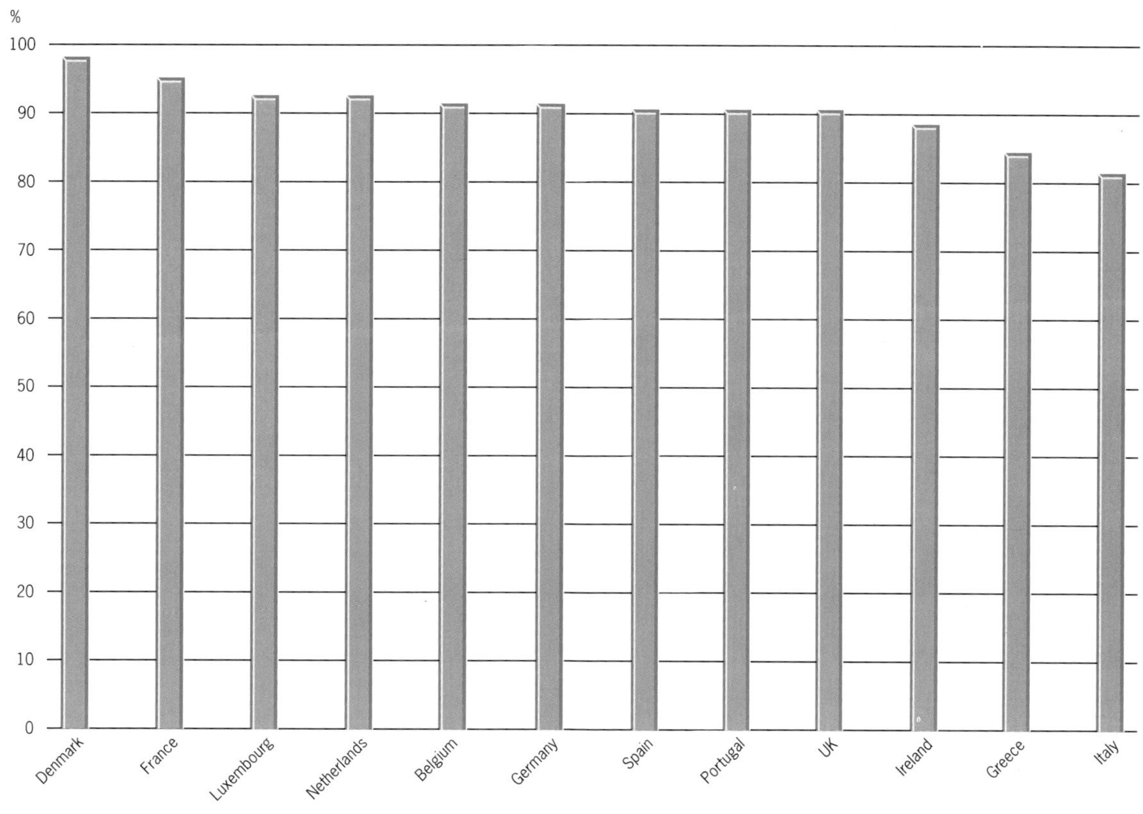

Source: 11th Annual Report on Monitoring the Application of Community Law (1993)

In many Western European regions, the volumes of waste disposed of are continuing to rise, despite recognition of the need to promote recycling, re-use and recovery programmes

Exhibit 13.7: Conformity of national measures implementing directives

Member state	European Commission comment on conformity (summarised)
Belgium	Distribution of power between regions can create difficulties. Particular problems in areas of waste, water and nature conservation
Denmark	No infringement proceedings for incorrect transposal. Excellent co-operation from Danish authorities
France	Incorrect or incomplete transposal on waste, water, nature conservation
Germany	Transposal of directives by circular poses problems
Greece	Often directly transposes directives into national law, though some are incorrectly transposed
Ireland	Problems in areas of environmental-impact assessment, waste, wildlife protection, protection from radiation
Italy	Problem areas include water, waste, laboratory animals, birds
Luxembourg	Good conformity record, with rare problem areas
Netherlands	Often imposes stricter measures than those imposed by directives. A few problems in areas of drinking water, wild birds
Portugal	Problem areas include air quality, waste, water
Spain	Problem areas include environmental-impact assessment, waste, nature conservation
UK	Problem areas include environmental-impact assessment, wild birds, air quality

Source: 11th Annual Report on Monitoring the Application of Community Law (1993)

There are marked variations between waste treatment capacity in states within Eastern Europe and those in the West

areas – wetlands, sites of scientific interest, nature reserves and so on – in various European countries and the percentage of territory these sites represent.

Waste

Waste disposal will become an increasingly significant problem for Eastern European countries as their economies grow. In many Western European regions, meanwhile, the volumes of waste disposed of are continuing to rise despite the longstanding recognition of the need to minimise waste and promote recycling, re-use and recovery programmes. The capacity for dealing with waste (whether solid or liquid) is patchy, and there are marked variations between waste treatment capacity in states within Eastern Europe and those in the West.

Recycling

Recycling rates provide an indication not only of public, corporate, and public sector environmental awareness but also of the degree to which the sophisticated systems for effective sorting, processing and sale of recycled material have been established in each country. (Exhibit 13.5 shows recycling rates for paper/cardboard and glass, and shows the significant variations in national performance and the scope for improvement throughout Europe.)

The regulatory and institutional framework

Research has shown that the need to comply with the law is the key driver in influencing company behaviour. Tougher regulatory standards and economic incentives (now increasingly enshrined by law) encourage companies to develop cleaner

Exhibit 13.8: Selected national initiatives

Belgium	Has made significant efforts to limit the polluting impact of vehicles. Has taken the lead in promoting eco-taxes at Community level, and has promoted fiscal measures to increase rates of better performing vehicles
Denmark	Heightened awareness of environmental issues, with good record of implementing EU measures. Has taken separate national initiatives (for example in the areas of food packaging, cadmium in phosphate fertilisers, carcinogenic substances; also a ban on CFCs) which frequently impose tighter restrictions than those introduced at Community level
France	Recent measures have been passed to promote work minimisation, recycling, re-use. Initiatives on packaging have been taken in advance of EU schemes. Public sector attention is given to opportunities from cleaner technologies
Germany	Environmental issues have a very high public profile, and there are strong consumer, political and environmental groups. Germany has occasionally set tighter demands than those imposed by the EU (for example concerning packaging and pentachlorophenol)
Greece	Previous rapid economic growth has placed constraints on Greece's natural resources. Urban pollution (particularly of air) is a significant issue
Ireland	There is a national action programme for the environment; also the recently established Environmental Protection Agency
Italy	Focus on improving the speed and effectiveness of implementing EU measures, as part of national administrative restructuring
Netherlands	Land use, reclamation and intensive agricultural practices are significant concerns, given the high population density and level of industrial development. Waste management is a priority issue. Innovative national environment plans seek to promote industrial and consumer involvement in promoting sustainable development. Several quasi-voluntary covenants have been agreed with industrial sectors (e.g. chemicals)
Portugal	The availability and quality of drinking water is a focus area. Environmental improvements are linked to infrastructure and economic development
Spain	Establishes national priorities from EU measures, often directly transposed into domestic law. Spain's autonomous communities have significant responsibilities for environmental regulation and monitoring
UK	National environmental policy framework, supported by annual progress reports. New systems of integrated pollution control and air pollution control being phased in. A unified environmental agency is being established

technologies and raise their standards of environmental performance. Regulation and its enforcement are also among the most important factors in determining location decisions.

A national and international agenda
A wide range of environmental laws now exist at national and international level. European Commission environmental measures currently number approximately 300, and the Fifth Environmental Action Programme sets an outline agenda for the next decade. In addition, a range of international conventions and agreements have been signed which also affect business. The OECD *Environmental Data Compendium* lists more than 60 such agreements.

Meanwhile individual countries have taken unilateral action to promote environmental protection; Scandinavian countries, for example, have been at the forefront of some of the most innovative environmental policy measures, notably those using economic instruments.

European Union environmental measures
The most significant body of environmental law is that initiated by the European Commission. The measures put forward not only have a bearing on where companies invest within the European Union, but are also increasingly influencing the prospects of companies investing outside the EU. Countries seeking EU membership are affected by EU measures too, and negotiate hard to ensure that environmental measures do not restrict trade or lead to competitive disadvantage.

In the countries of Eastern Europe, both the EU's means of policy formation and some of its standards are being adopted by governments developing their own national environmental policy framework.

Implementing legislation
The existence of this comprehensive body of environmental law does not necessarily mean that it is applied evenly, though there is little hard evidence to gauge the consistency or stringency of enforcement. In the European Union, the European Environment Agency (whose task it is to gather data on this type of issue) and the proposed Community-wide inspectorate (which will oversee the work of national environment inspectorates) will help to clarify how level the playing field is. An indication of national rates of progress in implementing EU environmental measures is provided in Exhibit 13.6. This shows that Italy and Greece have the poorest records, while the Danish record is the best.

Institutional and legal sophistication
The degree of institutional and legal sophistication varies considerably from one member state

Exhibit 13.9: Pollution abatement and control expenditure as percentage of GDP (for both public and private sectors in selected countries)

	1985	1987	1988	1989	1990
Austria	–	1.7	1.7	–	–
France	0.8	1.0	1.0	1.0	1.0
Germany	1.5	1.6	1.6	1.6	1.6
Netherlands	1.5	1.5	–	1.5	–
Portugal	–	–	–	0.6	–
UK	1.3	–	–	–	1.5

Source: OECD *Environmental Data Compendium* 1993

Scandinavian countries have been at the forefront of some of the most innovative policy measures, notably those using economic instruments

For particular industrial sectors, such as chemicals, hostility to new development is now a serious problem in many European regions

to the next. Broadly speaking, northern European states have long-established environmental institutions and a longer history of legislation to tackle industrial pollution. However, even the more advanced countries with international reputations for taking a tough line on environmental matters (such as Germany) can have difficulties in implementing environmental measures due to the nature of their administrative systems. The same is true of Belgium, where the federal nature of government creates difficulties in ensuring consistent application of the law. For new members of the European Union, some adjustments have to be made. In Sweden, for example, framework legislation is often supplementary noncompulsory guidelines, with compulsory limit values fixed through individually assessed permits. This approach may need adaptation, though it appears unlikely that there will be a problem for Sweden in meeting the standards required by EU measures.

Regional and national priorities for action

For member states, the body of EC environmental law ensures a degree of regulatory consistency and a common approach to regulation. However, a number of factors combine to create distinctive regimes within member states which can be of real significance when making location decisions. Exhibit 13.8 provides information on some of the key features of national environmental policies and priorities.

Environmental expenditure

The potential expenditure on tackling environmental problems and ensuring future sustainable growth in future is enormous. Public and private expenditure on pollution abatement and control

as a percentage of GDP has remained relatively steady in several European countries, as Exhibit 13.9 indicates.

Promoting environmental improvement through fiscal measures is one way in which national governments can confront the problems of financing environmental protection. Fiscal measures are used, or are being considered, to reduce carbon emissions (the proposed 'carbon tax'), to promote recycling (recycling credits in the UK, for example) and to influence consumption patterns. One area where this has been successfully implemented is in promoting the take-up of unleaded petrol: across Europe, it is now the norm for unleaded petrol to be cheaper per litre than leaded fuel. Exhibit 13.10 (below), which shows the market share of unleaded petrol in selected countries, illustrates the dramatic differences across Europe.

Public concern, public pressure

Public pressure has been and remains an important driver in influencing companies' environmental performance. Opposition to new industrial projects in many EU localities is well documented.

For particular industrial sectors, such as waste management and chemicals, hostility to new development is now a serious problem in many European regions. On a more positive note, consumer enthusiasm for green products can present companies with new opportunities.

Economic and environmental choices: what the public think

Opinion polls and surveys provide an indication of the extent to which the public are prepared to accept economic development at the expense of

Exhibit 13.10: Market share of unleaded fuel

% gross annual availability

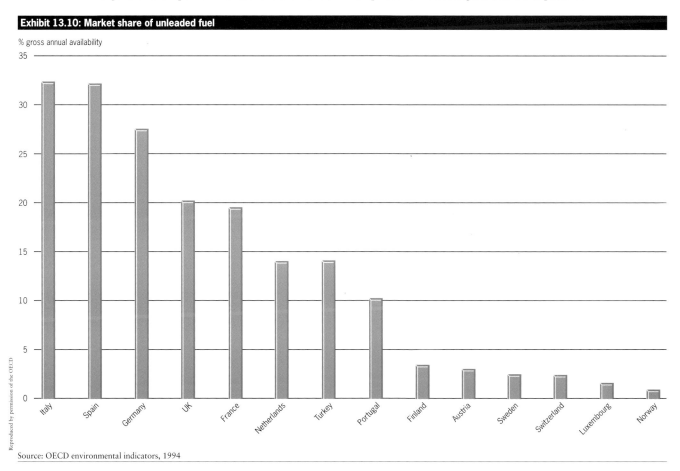

Source: OECD environmental indicators, 1994

Exhibit 13.11: Public opinion priorities for environmental protection and economic growth

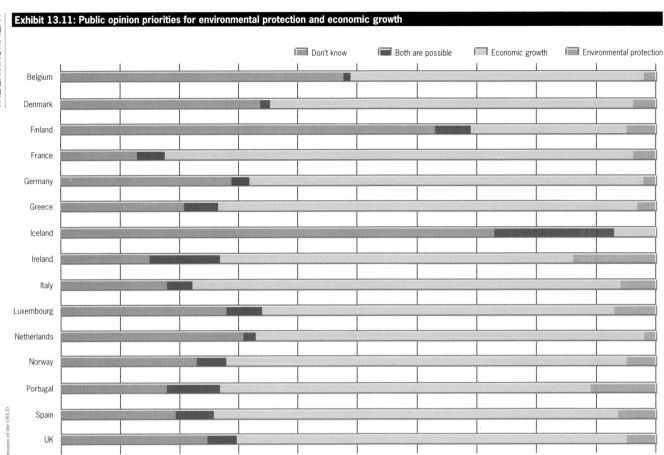

All figures 1992 except Finland (1989) and Norway (1990). Source: OECD *Environmental Data Compendium* 1993

Typically, Green parties throughout Europe have obtained between 3-5 per cent of the national vote, though higher figures have been reached in Germany

environmental protection in various locations. Exhibit 13.11 (above) compiles national responses to polls which examined whether priority should be given to environmental protection or economic development.

The degree to which there is consistency in the view that economic and environmental protection are both possible is worthy of note, and sends a significant message to business. It is also of interest that the greatest emphasis given to environmental protection is in Finland and Norway.

Pressure groups

Given the international sophistication of environmental pressure groups and their broad appeal, companies need to take account of their activities. Pressure groups have already been instrumental not only in the development of certain products, but also in monitoring corporate environmental performance, questioning claims about the life-cycle impact of products, probing the need for packaging and so on. In addition, pressure groups can on occasion wield significant political influence. In recognition of their influence, many firms are adopting a more open and interactive approach to communicating with these important stakeholders than they have done in the past.

The political power of the Greens

The political strength of the Green movement is a further indicator of the extent to which pressure may be placed on businesses to inject environ-

mental awareness into the corporate bloodstream. Although national electoral systems and traditions clearly have a significant influence on the electoral success of Green parties in different countries, it is worth noting that Green representation in local elections is often stronger than at national level, where electoral systems – either first-past-the-post or with electoral thresholds – can act against their national success. In Sweden, for example, the Green party holds more than 550 local council seats and 77 county council seats; in Finland, some 350 local council seats are held.

Pockets of political strength are a feature of Green politics: we see, for example, strong representation and activity in cities such as Gothenburg, Stockholm and Helsinki.

Typically, Green parties throughout Europe have obtained between 3-5 per cent of the national vote, though higher figures have been reached in Germany. Indeed, the continuing strength of the German Green Party is demonstrated by the fact that it has 12 members of the European Parliament out of the total German complement of 23.

In the countries of Eastern Europe, Green parties have featured among the early established political parties of the post-communist era. Although many of these organisations have faded away since initial elections or have been subsumed within larger political parties, there are still pockets of political strength, notably in Georgia, where three cabinet posts are currently held by members of the Green party.

Chapter 14

CORPORATE TAX

Corporate taxation in the New Europe is currently developing in at least three significant areas: the move towards harmonisation; the birth of tax regimes in the new nation states of Central and Eastern Europe (CEE); and the attempts of the more sophisticated regimes to come to terms with the ever-increasing complexity of modern commercial activity.

The long haul towards harmonisation

Competition for investment within Europe has produced a significant reduction in corporate tax rates in most countries, to the point where headline rates tend to fall in a fairly narrow range of 28-35 per cent. Europe may, however, have reached a point where internal political and revenue-raising pressures will slowly start to push rates upwards. It is also becoming questionable to what extent the member states of the Union are committed to harmonisation with regard to taxes, as evidenced by the recent demise of the draft directive that would have removed interest withholding taxes for transactions within the EU.

Tax regimes in Central and Eastern Europe

Due to the availability of natural resources and access to huge new markets, the Central/Eastern European region presents many new opportunities to the investor. Much Western advice has been offered to those states developing a national corporate tax system. However, the desire to attract investment is counterbalanced by a desire to prevent new-found wealth from draining out of the region. Add to this the lack of experience of some countries in administering a tax system, and a lack of familiarity with modern ways of doing business, and the CEE countries present a minefield for the unwary.

Coming to terms with ever-increasing complexity

As multinational corporations reorganise themselves along functional lines – in many cases leaving behind traditional notions of entity-based structures as new types of entity are developed for doing business and as tax planning becomes ever more complex – tax regimes around Europe are attempting to catch up with commercial reality at a variety of speeds.

With these factors in mind, it is evident that any investment decision requires detailed and specific analysis of the tax implications in each applicable jurisdiction. The purpose of this chapter is to give some indication of the factors which need to be taken into account when considering the potential tax costs and opportunities available in Europe.

Evaluating and ranking the corporate tax regimes across Europe is a complex task due to the number of factors that have an impact on the tax burden of companies.

In considering the overall impact of taxation it is also necessary to look at the tax burden on the investor: where the investor's return on an investment flows cross-border it is likely that additional tax costs will arise, in particular withholding taxes, in repatriating profits to the parent company's jurisdiction. Further tax cost may arise on distribution from the parent company to the individual investor. The combination of withholding taxes and the denial of access to tax credits arising from dividends means that in many circumstances the non-resident investor is at a disadvantage compared to the domestic investor.

The potential for double taxation which arises in such situations is one of the main reasons for the conclusion of double-tax treaties (in most cases bilateral, but occasionally embracing a larger number of territories). However, these treaties rarely succeed completely in removing bias against non-resident investors.

Because of the complexity of the position it is impossible to produce a comparative tax analysis that applies to all investors. However, in 1992 the London-based Institute of Fiscal Studies (IFS) published a model which provides a useful insight into the characteristics of some of the major Western European tax systems (the members of EFTA). The approach used is to calculate the pre-tax return required from an investment by a parent company through an overseas subsidiary to produce a 5 per cent post-tax return to the investor. The changes that have occurred since 1992 in the jurisdictions covered are in general not great enough to have a significant effect on the results of the IFS study. (These are shown in Exhibit 14.1.)

Elsewhere in this chapter we look at some of the key features of Europe's tax systems which must be taken into account when considering an investment opportunity in Europe, or when deciding where to locate a function that is not necessarily bound by geographical restrictions. These comments are broadened out to encompass some of the characteristics of the systems in Central and Eastern Europe which are not included in the IFS calculations. In order to illustrate some of the major issues, we have based our comments on investments made through a holding company resident in the same territory as the investor, with the foreign investment taking the form of a subsidiary or branch activity.

Basis of taxation in country of business activity
Tax rates
A simple review of national corporate tax rates applicable in each country gives a misleading picture of the total tax burden for a number of a

CORPORATE TAX

Reproduced by permission of the OECD

Exhibit 14.1: Required pre-tax rate of return to produce a 5% post-tax return to the investor, when the subsidiary is financed by one-third loans, one-third equity from the parent company and one-third retention by the subsidiary

Investment in:	Investment from: Austria	Investment from: Belgium	Investment from: Denmark
Austria		6.8	6.9
Belgium	6.6	-	6.9
Denmark	6.3	6.8	
Finland	6.6	6.4	6.1
France	6.8	6.3	6.1
Germany	10.9	8.0	7.8
Greece	8.6	6.9	9.9
Ireland	6.5	6.8	6.9
Italy	7.7	7.5	8.1
Luxembourg	6.4	6.5	6.7
Netherlands	6.3	6.2	6.4
Norway	8.0	7.3	8.5
Portugal	7.0	6.8	6.9
Spain	6.6	6.7	6.9
Sweden	6.5	6.6	6.3
Switzerland	6.2	6.4	6.3
UK	6.1	6.0	6.1

Investment in:	Investment from: Japan	Investment from: Luxembourg	Investment from: The Netherlands	Investment from: Norway
Austria	7.7	7.2	6.4	6.6
Belgium	8.1	6.6	6.1	6.4
Denmark	7.2	6.6	5.9	5.6
Finland	7.4	7.0	5.9	5.8
France	7.3	6.6	6.2	5.6
Germany	8.3	7.1	7.6	5.2
Greece	8.7	6.7	6.5	6.4
Ireland	7.7	7.3	6.9	7.2
Italy	7.8	8.3	8.7	7.1
Luxembourg	8.5		6.3	6.6
Netherlands	7.6	6.9		6.6
Norway	7.8	8.8	8.9	
Portugal	14.5	10.2	11.9	7.0
Spain	7.6	6.9	6.4	6.7
Sweden	7.5	7.1	6.1	5.9
Switzerland	7.5	7.6	6.1	6.1
UK	7.3	6.6	6.2	6.1

Source: OECD/IFS

reasons. Many countries impose local profit-based tax charges in addition to the national levy. In Switzerland, for example, the maximum federal rate of taxation is only 9.8 per cent, but the Swiss cantons levy their own tax at rates varying from 10 to 27 per cent. Other countries with significant local tax charges are Italy and Germany. Determination of the effective rate is complicated by the fact that some of these local taxes are deductible from profits in calculating the national tax charge.

In addition, a number of countries have introduced a temporary surtax (a percentage of the national tax charge); these include Belgium and Turkey, and also Germany, where a 'solidarity' surcharge has been introduced to help fund some of the costs of reunification.

Not all countries have a single corporate income tax rate. In the United Kingdom, for example, a lower rate applies up to a maximum level of taxable profit, whilst in the Netherlands a higher rate applies to the first slice of profits. Romania has a more complex banding system. In Tajikistan, meanwhile, the standard corporate income tax rate of 45 per cent is raised to 80 or 90 per cent for profits exceeding a stated 'maximum level of profitability'.

In Belgium and some Central and Eastern European countries, high rates apply to foreign branch profits (though these may be reduced under a relevant double-tax treaty). Germany is unique in Europe in having different rates for distributed and undistributed profits.

Tax rates may also vary for different types of specific incentives offered to encourage particular types of investment. For example, Ireland offers a tax rate of 10 per cent in respect of manufacturing companies and also for certain types of financial services companies operating in the Custom House Dock area of Dublin. In southern Italy, many manufacturing companies are exempt from corporate income tax (IRPEG) for a 10-year period, and from local income tax (ILOR) for 10 years from the first year in which they make a profit.

Tax holidays of varying lengths are available to foreign investors in certain industry sectors in the CEE countries (principally labour-intensive manufacturing operations). For instance, some countries in the region have lower tax rates for enterprises with foreign participation in excess of a specified level (usually 30 per cent) and higher rates for specified activities (such as intermediary activities, banking and insurance services, and casinos).

Tax rates may vary for different types of profit or gain. Many countries tax capital gains at a different rate from recurring profits. In France, for example, the rate of tax on gains depends on how long the asset has been held.

In Germany, a 'solidarity' surcharge has been introduced to help fund some of the costs of reunification

Investment from: Finland	Investment from: France	Investment from: Germany	Investment from: Greece	Investment from: Ireland	Investment from: Italy
7.3	7.9	7.4	6.2	5.6	7.1
7.0	7.3	6.3	5.3	5.7	7.3
6.6	6.7	6.3	6.6	5.4	6.7
	7.2	5.4	6.0	5.7	6.1
6.4		5.2	6.0	5.4	6.6
8.1	8.1		4.8	6.2	9.9
7.5	11.1	6.7		9.7	7.5
7.0	7.7	6.6	12.7		6.8
8.0	10.2	5.4	7.4	10.4	
7.0	7.3	6.6	6.5	5.6	7.1
6.7	7.2	6.6	5.7	5.5	6.2
8.4	7.9	6.2	22.1	5.9	7.7
7.3	7.9	6.6	11.7	9.0	7.1
7.2	7.5	6.6	6.6	7.0	7.0
6.6	6.9	6.5	6.1	5.5	6.9
6.9	7.2	6.5	5.6	5.5	6.9
6.7	7.2	6.0	5.9	7.3	6.0

Investment from: Portugal	Investment from: Spain	Investment from: Sweden	Investment from: Switzerland	Investment from: UK	Investment from: US
7.1	7.3	5.5	6.2	6.8	6.7
7.4	7.9	5.9	6.1	6.5	6.9
5.6	5.6	5.5	5.7	6.0	6.5
6.8	5.3	5.4	6.1	5.9	6.5
6.6	7.5	5.2	6.0	6.5	6.4
8.5	8.2	6.4	7.4	7.1	7.8
8.8	9.3	6.5	6.9	7.3	10.1
15.3	15.6	6.5	7.0	7.6	6.8
7.9	9.1	9.1	9.7	9.6	8.1
7.9	7.3	5.7	8.3	6.3	6.7
8.8	7.3	5.4	5.9	6.3	6.6
7.1	9.3	5.6	9.5	6.6	7.8
	7.3	11.1	6.6	7.2	13.2
6.0		5.9	6.4	6.9	6.
7.7	7.2		6.0	6.2	6.5
7.0	7.2	5.6		6.2	6.5
6.7	7.1	5.6	6.0		6.4

Very high rates of capital allowances may be available as a special incentive to encourage investment in depressed areas or in certain types of asset

Corporate income tax is not, of course, the only source of fiscal expense experienced by companies operating within Europe. Net worth taxes, VAT and import taxes also play an important part in any investment decision. In Kazakhstan, for instance, import duties may be as high as 300 per cent of the customs value of goods imported.

Tax base

In order to obtain a meaningful estimate of the actual tax burden that will be borne by a business, it is necessary to take into account the different ways of calculating the tax base (taxable profits) in each country.

Most European systems take accounting profit as their starting-point for calculating taxable profits. Adjustments are then made to deny relief for certain revenue expenses and, where relief is available for capital expenditure, to ensure that amortisation is allowable on a uniform basis for various classes of asset.

Most regimes deny relief for a certain amount of revenue expenditure on 'non-business' items such as entertaining. Some Central and Eastern European countries impose additional restrictions on deductions for salaries and interest expense on long-term loans, although protection against such restrictions is sometimes afforded by double-tax treaties.

Relief for capital expenditure varies widely, particularly with respect to intangibles. Purchased goodwill, for example, is not deductible at all in the United Kingdom, whereas Germany permits amortisation over 15 years.

The IFS model assumes investment in three types of capital assets – that is, plant and machinery, commercial and industrial buildings, and inventory. Some countries, such as Belgium, allow tax depreciation for all three types of asset. Invariably, countries will allow some depreciation on plant and machinery, and generally also in industrial buildings, though at lower rates. Ireland and the UK do not generally allow tax depreciation on commercial buildings.

The basis for computing depreciation allowances is generally straight-line (that is, in equal amounts) for buildings. For plant and machinery, both declining-balance (a fixed percentage of a reducing amount) and straight-line methods are used; sometimes, as in France, the opportunity to switch from one to the other is available.

Very high rates of capital allowances may be available as a special incentive to encourage investment in depressed areas (100 per cent for enterprise zones in the United Kingdom, for example) or in certain types of asset (up to 70 per cent in Turkey). A number of countries offer special incentives for research and development.

Another important area is the taxation of foreign exchange differences. Clearly, cross-border investment can give rise to considerable foreign exchange risk which the investor may or may not choose to hedge at any one of a number of levels. The tax treatment of differences arising varies widely across Europe.

Aside from accounting profit-based calculations of tax, a number of countries offer a special regime for various types of group service company. Service centres (providing, for example, accounting and administration services) may often, in countries such as Belgium and the Netherlands, be subject to tax on a fixed mark-up on the costs they incur (perhaps 5 or 10 per cent). Treasury management/group finance companies may also be able to negotiate a tax base restricted to a small percentage spread on funds borrowed and on-lent.

Another factor that could have a significant impact on the final tax burden of an enterprise is the facility for the offset of losses incurred in prior or future periods. Few countries allow losses to be carried back for offset against profits of prior years. Exceptions include Ireland (one year), Germany (two years) and France, the Netherlands and the UK (three years).

Most countries allow a limited period for the carrying forward of losses (after which any unused losses expire). Belgium, Germany, Ireland, Norway, Sweden and the UK are among those countries where losses may be carried forward indefinitely.

Another area of wide variation is the possibility of offsetting the losses of one company against the profits of other group companies resident in the same country. This tends to be a feature of the more sophisticated jurisdictions and may take the form of fiscal consolidation (as, for example, in France and Germany), the ability to 'surrender' losses (as in the UK) or the potential for making equalisation payment (such as Finland's 'group contributions'). Italy is notable for being a Western system which has no such facilities, while Denmark, at the other end of the scale, is the only European country that permits foreign associates to be consolidated for tax purposes. The proposed EC directive on cross-border loss relief aims to make this the rule rather than the exception, but the original deadline for the directive coming into force (1 January 1993) has now long since been passed and its current stage of development is unknown.

Tax cost of profit repatriation
Distribution of profit to overseas parent
There are two main types of system for the taxation of distributed profits:

- The classical system;
- The imputation system.

Under the classical system, the shareholder receives no credit for the tax paid on the profits out of which the dividend was paid. Effectively, therefore, double taxation is suffered, once at the paying company level and once at the shareholder level. Countries which apply the classical system include the Netherlands and Luxembourg.

The alternative is the imputation system, under which the shareholder is entitled to a tax credit representing the corporate tax borne on the profits out of which the dividend was paid. This credit may be set against the shareholder's own tax liability on the dividend. Examples of countries which use the imputation system are the UK, France, Germany and Italy.

It is rare for tax credits arising under an imputation system to be available to non-resident parent companies. The UK is the only imputation system country which has regularly included in its double-tax agreements provisions for non-resident companies to recover a proportion of the tax credit arising from dividends paid by UK subsidiaries. It is generally the position, therefore, that non-resident shareholders are at a disadvantage compared to resident shareholders under the imputation system.

In addition, all countries apart from Albania, Croatia, Hungary, Ireland, Latvia, Lithuania and the UK impose a withholding tax on dividends paid to a non-resident parent company, though such withholding taxes may be reduced or eliminated by a double-tax agreement.

A recent EC directive known as the Parent/ Subsidiary Directive abolishes withholding taxes on dividends paid from one member state to another where the recipient company owns at least 25 per cent of the capital of the payer. An important exception to the rule concerns Germany, which will retain the right to levy a 5 per cent dividend withholding tax until 30 June 1996.

In situations where the local business is operated through a branch of the foreign company, a number of countries (including the CEE countries, France and Spain) impose a withholding tax on branch remittances. Again, these may be reduced or eliminated by treaty but they are not covered by the Parent/Subsidiary Directive.

Whether the investment is structured through a branch or a company, it may be possible to repatriate funds in forms other than dividends or branch remittances. Debt financing may permit some funds to return to the home jurisdiction in the form of interest. This may be beneficial in terms of providing interest deductions in the foreign country (provided these outweigh the tax cost of corresponding interest receipts in the home country) and allowing access to lower rates of withholding tax. Because of the evident scope for abuse, most countries have introduced rules which have the effect of recharacterising interest payments as dividends where the rate of interest is higher than at 'arm's length' rate or where the ratio of debt to equity in the company is seen to be excessive. The precise rules differ widely, but many countries have statutory debt-to-equity ratios for foreign-related party borrowing. These range from 1.5:1 in France to 9:1 for holding companies in Germany.

Countries without such specific 'thin capitalisation' rules usually have general anti-abuse rules which are capable of application to similar situations, although in countries such as Italy these tend to allow much greater planning flexibility.

Taxation at parent company level
In some countries, for example Luxembourg and the Netherlands, foreign dividend income is excluded from tax (as is any gain on the disposal of the underlying investment) provided certain conditions relating to the nature of the investment are satisfied. Other countries, such as

Denmark is the only European country that permits foreign associates to be consolidated for tax purposes... The proposed EC directive on cross-border relief aims to make this the rule rather than the exception

Belgium and France, will exempt a proportion of the dividend from tax. Alternatively, countries such as the UK will tax dividends but will allow a credit for the tax paid on profits in the subsidiary jurisdiction out of which the dividend was paid. Thus relief will be available for underlying tax as well as for any withholding tax.

These arrangements for avoiding the double taxation of profits will be enshrined either in domestic legislation or in double-tax treaty arrangements between the countries concerned. Each country has developed its own methods for calculating double-tax relief. These are affected by such factors as whether or not relief is calculated by reference to accounting or tax profits in the subsidiary's jurisdiction, whether there is any overall limit on double-tax relief in the parent company jurisdiction, and whether relief is calculated by aggregating the foreign source income of the parent or on a source-by-source basis.

Over recent years, a number of countries have introduced special regimes for international holding companies. One of the newest is in the United Kingdom. Although this regime does not provide for exemption from UK tax for foreign income, it does attempt to remove some of the difficulties that are posed to UK companies with significant foreign income by the UK's advance corporation tax (ACT) rules.

Return to individual investor

The difference made by the final step – the return of the income generated by the investment to the original source of the funding – depends largely on whether the parent company jurisdiction operates an imputation system on paying dividends to individual shareholders. Some systems, for example in the Netherlands, do not impute any part of the parent company tax as a credit to a resident shareholder while, for example, Germany, France and the UK do.

Those countries that operate an imputation system only grant a tax credit from an income source which has borne corporate income tax or distribution taxes. The UK, while granting a tax credit, requires ACT to be paid in respect of the dividend. In the past, the extent to which this ACT represented a further cost to the distributing company depended on its capacity to offset ACT against its mainstream corporation tax liability. These types of rules make distribution of profits from foreign source income less attractive than distributions from domestic source profits. In the UK, for example, the Foreign Income Dividend (FID) legislation introduced in 1994 has has gone some way towards addressing the problem by providing for refunds of ACT in situations where double-tax relief leaves no tax against which to offset ACT.

Certainty of tax treatment

All investment decisions are ultimately based on a consideration of the twin factors of risk and return. An examination of the interaction of the relevant domestic tax systems, as affected by the application of double-tax treaties and European Union directives, is essential in estimating post-tax returns.

Also important, however, is the assessment of risk. This can, of course, include the risk that the tax authorities of a particular jurisdiction will not interpret the facts or legal implications of the investment in the same way as the investor or as another jurisdiction.

One way of reducing this risk is to operate in countries that have signed bilateral double-tax treaties. As well as providing relief from double taxation – typically by allocating taxing rights for cross-border transactions, reducing maximum rates of withholding tax and setting out methods of providing double-tax relief – these also lay out a framework for the settling of disputes and, through the OECD Model Convention on which most modern double-tax agreements (DTAs) are based, represent a move towards a standardisation of tax principles. Consequently, the investor is assured greater certainty of treatment.

The other major factor contributing to certainty of treatment is the consistency of local revenue authorities and their willingness to agree with the taxpayer prior to a transaction the tax treatment that will be applicable to it. The Netherlands is at one end of the scale; the tax authorities there have wide powers to give advance rulings on proposed treatments, including incentive-type treatments, which give a binding guarantee of tax treatment to the taxpayer. In the middle are countries such as the UK, which give binding rulings only in respect of certain specific types of transaction but which are generally helpful in indicating to the taxpayer how they will seek to interpret statutory tax provisions. At the other end of the scale comes Russia, which issues no binding advance clearances and rarely meet its statutory obligations to respond to queries about interpretation of statute.

Of the major CEE nations, Hungary, the Slovak Republic, Bulgaria and Poland stand out as jurisdictions in which it is possible to obtain advance clearance in certain issues – for example, qualification for special incentives (though Bulgaria and Poland have now ceased to offer these to foreign investors). In contrast, the Czech Republic, Romania and Slovenia are among those which do not issue clearances. All of the CEE jurisdictions mentioned here are generally willing to supply non-binding rulings.

Finally, no survey of tax issues in Europe would be complete without a mention of transfer pricing. Not surprisingly, tax authorities throughout Europe are becoming increasingly sensitive to the artificial movement of profits between jurisdictions by the manipulation of prices for the transfer of goods and the provision of services by one group company to another in a different jurisdiction. The publication of the first part of the new OECD draft report on transfer pricing has gone some way to highlight these issues.

Most European systems have either specific transfer-pricing legislation or more flexible anti-abuse provisions, and there is a perceptible increase in their use by the authorities. Spain, for example, has recently imposed its first major transfer-pricing adjustment on a multinational company.

Faced with varying interpretations of such legislation and the variety of methods that may be utilised to establish an 'arm's-length' price, the increasing availability of advance pricing agreement (APA) mechanisms is to be welcomed. Spain, for instance, is due to implement APA procedures in 1996, and this trend is also visible in other sophisticated jurisdictions.

The increasing availability of advance pricing agreement mechanisms is to be welcomed

Chapter 15

EXPATRIATE ISSUES

As companies exercise their greater freedom to move personnel across Europe, the issues surrounding these transfers become increasingly important. In this chapter we examine some of the expatriate issues that need to be considered, including: personal taxation, general cost of living and accommodation costs in the country in question, the availability of international schools, general healthcare costs and levels of crime.

Taxation

Much has been written about the harmonisation of laws and policies within Europe. The one common approach adopted by all countries is that they all impose taxes and social security on employees and employers. That is, however, as far as harmonisation goes where income taxes are concerned. Each country has its own tax

time limits. Belgium, for instance, allows deductions of up to BEF1,200,000 (approximately US$41,000) for executives employed at a headquarters or research centre, but the application must be made within six months of the executive's arrival in the country.

In addition to income tax considerations, social security within Europe is also an important – and usually costly – issue. Each country imposes its own rates and limits, and these vary considerably. In general, an individual pays a contribution in the country in which he or she is working. For example, France and Italy have varying rates depending on the individual's job.

All 17 member states of the European Economic Area are covered by a single treaty; the EU social security legislation thus covers all nationals of the Union who are working in

> With the increase in labour mobility throughout Europe, many countries have special expatriate regimes which grant concessions to foreign nationals

Exhibit 15.1: Maximum income tax rates for selected European countries and the US							
	Top tax rate assuming married taxpayer (%)						
	1988	1989	1990	1991	1992	1993	1994
Austria	62	50	50	50	50	50	50
Belgium	75	59	59	59	59	60	60
Denmark	68	68	68	68	68	68	65
Finland	67	60	59	59	57	57	57
France	57	57	57	57	58	59	59
Germany	56	56	53	55	55	53	53
Ireland	58	56	56	52	48	48	48
Italy	62	50	50	50	51	51	51
Luxembourg	56	56	56	50	60	51	51
Netherlands	72	72	60	60	60	60	60
Norway	55	55	52	50	41	42	42
Portugal	–	–	–	40	40	40	40
Spain	56	56	56	56	56	56	56
Sweden	75	72	65	50	50	50	50
Switzerland*	48	48	48	48	48	48	48
UK	40	40	40	40	40	40	40
US**	28	28	28	28	31	40	40

*Federal and Geneva Canton. **Federal rates, only for a married taxpayer. Source: Ernst & Young

laws, tax base and tax rates. This leads to significant differences in the level of tax imposed on any given income. General maximum tax rates imposed range from 40-70 per cent, though top rates have largely been reduced over recent years.

With the increase in labour mobility throughout Europe, many countries have special expatriate regimes which grant concessions to foreign nationals assigned to that country by their employer. Historically, these concessions have been seen as a means of reducing costs in order to attract business. Such concessions can offer considerable tax savings. The countries that provide expatriate concessions include Spain, Denmark, France, the Netherlands, Belgium, Switzerland and the UK. In many cases, however, certain restrictions apply, and application for the concessions often has to be made within strict

another member country. However, the rules are more complex where the employee is assigned overseas by his or her employer. In certain circumstances it is possible for an employee to remain in his or her home country scheme for up to five years, provided the contract of employment remains with the home country employer.

These special rules cover three particular circumstances. An employee assigned overseas within the EEA for a period of less than 12 months will, provided certain conditions are met, automatically remain in his or her home scheme, though an application needs to be made to achieve this position. An employee working in more than one member state can also remain in his or her home scheme for at least five years – perhaps longer if he or she continues to remain habitually resident in his/her home country.

Exhibit 15.2: Net-to-gross income comparison for married person with two children, earning £50,000 net, 1995

Country	Net	Social security	Tax	Pension	Gross
Austria	50,000	5,195	22,786		77,981
Belgium	50,000	15,553	49,783		115,336
Denmark	50,000	7,292	64,253		121,545
Finland	50,000	4,041	64,818		118,859
France	50,000	13,473	9,717	1,708	74,898
Germany	50,000	6,653	19,236		75,889
Greece	50,000	2,974	29,162		82,136
Ireland	50,000	3,181	37,127		90,308
Italy	50,000	8,319	29,777		88,096
Luxembourg	50,000	5,139	18,618		73,757
Netherlands	50,000	2,773	49,878	4,882	107,533
Norway	50,000	6,863	31,127		87,990
Portugal	50,000	9,763	26,273		86,036
Spain	50,000	1,370	34,909		86,279
Sweden	50,000	0	45,710		95,710
Switzerland	50,000	5,010	8,153	3,103	66,266
UK	50,000	1,999	25,621		77,620
US	50,000	3,470	13,105		66,575
US (New York)	50,000	3,613	22,822		76,435

Source: Ernst & Young

Exhibit 15.3: Net-to-gross income comparison for married person with two children earning £100,00 net, 1995

Country	Net	Social security	Tax	Pension	Gross
Austria	100,000	5,195	61,618		166,813
Belgium	100,000	34,324	124,627		258,951
Denmark	100,000	16,036	151,240		267,276
Finland	100,000	21,406	133,433		254,839
France	100,000	27,019	74,369	4,715	206,103
Germany	100,000	6,653	72,166		178,819
Greece	100,000	3,522	70,071		173,593
Ireland	100,000	5,443	85,368		190,811
Italy	100,000	8,806	77,714		186,520
Luxembourg	100,000	5,134	71,182		176,316
Netherlands	100,000	2,773	124,878	4,882	232,533
Norway	100,000	14,586	72,414		187,000
Portugal	100,000	20,807	62,859		183,666
Spain	100,000	1,370	98,545		199,915
Sweden	100,000	0	98,680		198,680
Switzerland	100,000	11,942	38,630	3,103	153,675
UK	100,000	1,999	58,954		160,953
US	100,000	4,594	39,472		144,066
US (New York)	100,000	4,946	63,446		168,392

Source: Ernst & Young

Exhibit 15.4: Net-to-gross income comparison for married person with two children earning £150,000 net, 1995

Country	Net	Social Security	Tax	Pension	Gross
Austria	150,000	5,195	100,453		255,648
Belgium	150,000	53,094	199,471		402,565
Denmark	150,000	24,780	238,225		413,005
Finland	150,000	32,828	207,991		390,819
France	150,000	36,336	146,997	7,794	341,127
Germany	150,000	6,653	128,542		285,195
Greece	150,000	4,071	110,980		265,051
Ireland	150,000	7,704	133,610		291,314
Italy	150,000	8,806	129,754		288,560
Luxembourg	150,000	5,134	123,746		278,880
Netherlands	150,000	2,773	199,877	4,882	357,532
Norway	150,000	22,308	113,702		286,010
Portugal	150,000	31,852	99,444		281,296
Spain	150,000	1,370	162,182		313,552
Sweden	150,000	0	150,990		300,990
Switzerland	150,000	19,582	77,330	3,103	250,015
UK	150,000	1,999	92,287		244,286
US	150,000	5,814	72,460		228,274
US (New York)	150,000	6,379	110,840		267,219

Source: Ernst & Young

In order to prevent some of the more common personal and financial problems arising, many companies offer expatriate packages

Exhibit 15.5: Cost of living index (Zurich = 100)

Location	
Zurich	100
Oslo	95.8
Geneva	94.9
Copenhagen	92.0
Paris	87.0
Stockholm	85.2
Moscow	82.8
Frankfurt	79.8
Hamburg	79.7
Düsseldorf	79.4
Helsinki	79.3
Berlin	78.9
Lyon	78.9
Vienna	77.0
Luxembourg	75.2
London	74.1
Brussels	72.0
Milan	70.4
Amsterdam	70.3
Barcelona	69.5
Rome	68.0
Madrid	63.5
Dublin	62.6
Athens	56.7
Lisbon	55.9
Warsaw	44.5
Budapest	43.4
Belgrade	43.0
Prague	34.8

Source: *Prices and Earnings Around the Globe*, Union Bank of Switzerland 1994

Exhibit 15.6: Availability of international schools in European countries

	No. of international schools
Albania	1
Austria	5
Belgium	12
Bulgaria	1
Croatia	1
Czech Republic	2
Denmark	5
Finland	4
France	18
Germany	15
Greece	8
Hungary	3
Ireland	4
Italy	28
Latvia	1
Lithuania	1
Luxembourg	2
Netherlands	22
Norway	6
Poland	3
Portugal	12
Romania	1
Russia	3
Serbia	1
Slovakia	1
Slovenia	1
Spain	41
Sweden	6
Switzerland	35
Turkey	15
UK	26

Source: Specialist Publishing Services/*International Schools Directory* 1994/95

Finally, if it is in the employee's best interests to remain in his or her home scheme (for example, if he or she is soon to retire), or if he or she has special skills, an application can be made to remain in the home scheme for up to five years.

Exhibits 15.2, 15.3 and 15.4 take into account tax and social security rules to give gross-to-net salary comparisons for selected countries. These comparisons do not take into account differences in the cost of living in each location, nor any additional contributions paid by the employer.

The expatriate package

In order to prevent some of the more common personal and financial problems arising, many companies offer expatriate packages. These may be tailored to individual companies within the group, but the lack of an overall policy may lead to problems, most notably:

● Duplication of effort;
● Lack of consistency of approach;
● Key issues overlooked (pensions etc);
● Delay in implementation of transfer;
● Inadequate briefing of expatriates (about local customs, culture etc);
● Lack of contingency plans;
● Expatriates from different countries being offered different packages;
● Failure to capitalise on tax-effective planning.

In many cases it is therefore desirable to adopt an expatriate package which not only addresses issues such as length of assignment and remuneration, but which also looks at the individual's income tax position. The package should take into account the needs both of the company and the individual, as well as the long-term objectives of all parties. For the company, important considerations typically include:

● Legal aspects;
● Equal treatment;
● Ease of communication;
● Ease of administration;
● Flexibility;
● Future needs;
● Motivation;
● Value for money.

The employee will have a different set of needs, which will include:

● Destination;
● Departure date;
● Duration;
● Remuneration package, including cost of living and overseas allowances;
● Housing and schooling in the host country;
● Income tax equalisation;
● Subsequent career objectives.

Expatriate assignments usually fall into one of three categories: short-term (up to 12 months); mid-length (two to five years); and long-term (several years). Whilst a relocation policy is commonly utilised for short- and medium-term assignments, expatriates who become long-term assignees increasingly find that companies are reducing overseas allowances or 'localising' them.

The trend is towards a reduction in overseas mobility premiums and cost of living allowances, combined with an increase in healthcare, education and familiarisation programmes. A typical expatriate policy encompasses:

● An adjustment to home salary, to compensate

The expatriate package should take into account the needs both of the company and the individual, as well as the long-term objectives of all parties

Social security within Europe is an important – and usually costly – issue

Exhibit 15.7: Percentage of individuals experiencing selected crimes in 1988 and/or 1991

	Theft of/ from cars %	Home burglary %	Robbery and pickpockets %	Sexual incidents%
Belgium	5.0	2.2	2.3	2.3
Finland	4.5	0.6	2.4	2.5
Former Czechoslovakia	8.9	4.3	3.9	4.7
Former West Germany	6.3	1.3	2.0	4.4
France	9.9	2.4	2.2	2.5
Italy	10.9	2.4	2.7	1.6
Netherlands	8.1	2.2	2.7	4.5
Norway	4.8	0.8	1.0	4.0
Poland	12.8	2.3	7.8	5.6
Spain	16.5	1.7	5.0	4.1
Sweden	6.7	1.4	1.1	3.0
Switzerland	2.4	1.0	2.0	2.0
UK:				
England and Wales	12.0	2.5	2.1	3.5
Northern Ireland	7.7	1.1	1.2	6.3
Scotland	8.9	2.0	1.4	2.1
Japan	2.1	0.9	0.0	0.7
US	11.0	3.5	2.5	6.3

Source: Home Office, *International Crime Survey* 1994

for assignment country's tax and social security contributions;
● A cost of living or disturbance allowance (more than 75 per cent of employers pay a cost of living allowance; over 70 per cent use external consultants to establish allowances);
● Housing and utility allowance. Nearly all employers provide assistance in finding housing in the country of assignment; almost 70 per cent of employers limit the level of housing assistance; and almost 75 per cent allow expatriates to contribute to obtain a higher standard of housing;
● Education allowance. Registration and tuition fees of assignee's children are usually paid;
● Healthcare. The assignee and family are generally covered by medical insurance;
● Home leave. The airfare for an annual trip home for assignee and family is also fairly standard policy.

The cost of living
The kind of remuneration packages that companies need to pay to expatriate workers is strongly influenced by the prevailing cost of living and the level of real wages in the locality concerned. Living costs can vary considerably, even within one country. Exhibit 15.5 provides a broad picture, using Zurich as the base.

International schools
Another major concern for an expatriate is the availability of international schools. Each European country operates its own national education system, and there is little uniformity between them. Due to the growing number of expatriates, however, most countries now have schools specifically designed for the international community. Exhibit 15.6 outlines the number of international schools (which are members of the European Council of International Schools) in each country. The data is not comprehensive, but provides an approximate guide to the number of places available in each country. Most of these international schools offer a wide choice of curricula, including British, American or the International Baccalaureate, created to provide a common curriculum at upper secondary level and a matriculation examination with wide acceptability.

State education is free in all European countries and is generally compulsory from the ages of five or six and 16. A range of private (non-state) schools can also be found.

The question of crime
It is not always possible to compare crime figures directly, since each country has its own system of classifying and recording offences. It should also be noted that crime tends to be localised, with the result that two areas in the same town can have very different crime profiles. Police statistics do not present the full picture. The *International Crime Survey*, which asks the public directly about their experiences of crime over the past year, provides a better comparison across countries. This is illustrated in Exhibits 15.7 and 15.8.

Crime in Eastern Europe is a growing concern. However, many countries in the region have placed great emphasis on containing crime levels. It should be noted that crime levels in the former USSR are noticeably below those in many Western countries, though theft and robbery occur frequently in the major cities, with wealthy expatriates often the target.

Exhibit 15.8: Overall victimisation rates (all crimes)

27.5 -30%	Netherlands, US
25-27.4%	Poland
22.5-24.9%	England, former Czechoslovakia, Italy, Spain
20-22.4%	Former West Germany, Sweden
17.5-19.9%	France, Scotland, Belgium, Finland
15-17.4%	Norway, Switzerland
12.5-14.9%	North Ireland
<12.4%	Japan

Source: Home Office, *International Crime Survey* 1994

Exhibit 15.9: Crime rates in Eastern Europe per 100,000 inhabitants, 1993

	Murder	All crime
Armenia	0.6	23.3
Belarus	0.5	58.3
Moldova	0.7	69.3
Russia	1.2	113.1
Ukraine	0.5	58.1

Source: *Russian and Eurasia Facts and Figures Annual* Vol. 19, 1994

Expatriates who become long-term assignees increasingly find that companies are reducing overseas allowances or 'localising' them